The Frazzled Teacher's Wellness Plan

The Frazzled Teacher's Wellness Plan

*A Five Step Program
for Reclaiming Time, Managing Stress,
and Creating a Healthy Lifestyle*

J. Allen Queen ⋆ Patsy S. Queen

CORWIN PRESS, INC.
A Sage Publications Company
Thousand Oaks, California

The content of this book has been carefully researched, reviewed, and edited for accuracy, but it is for reference and informational purposes only. Under no circumstances should the information in this book be used to diagnose or treat any health or medical condition. Only a doctor can diagnose and treat health and medical conditions. The authors, editors, and publisher recommend that health and medical problems always be referred to the school nurse, family physician, or hospital immediately. The authors and publishers disclaim all responsibility for any liability, loss, injury, or damage incurred as a consequence, directly or indirectly, of the use and application of any of the information in this book.

For information:

Corwin Press
A Sage Publications Company
2455 Teller Road
Thousand Oaks, California 91320
www.corwinpress.com

Sage Publications Ltd.
6 Bonhill Street
London EC2A 4PU
United Kingdom

Sage Publications India Pvt. Ltd.
B-42, Panchsheel Enclave
Post Box 4109
New Delhi 110 017 India

Printed in the United States of America

Library of Congress Cataloging-in-Publication Data

Queen, J. Allen.
The frazzled teacher's wellness plan : a five step program for reclaiming time, managing stress, and creating a healthy lifestyle / by J. Allen Queen and Patsy S. Queen.
    p. cm.
Includes bibliographical references.
ISBN 0-7619-2961-4 (cloth : acid-free paper) -- ISBN 0-7619-2962-2 (pbk. : acid-free paper)
    1. Teachers—Health and hygiene—United States. 2. Teachers—Job stress—United States.
3. Teachers—Time management—United States. 4. Stress management—United States.
I. Queen, Patsy S. II. Title.
LB3415.Q84 2004
613.7′024′372—dc22

                                        2003016581

This book is printed on acid-free paper.

        04   05   06   07   7   6   5   4   3   2

Acquisitions Editor:	Faye Zucker
Editorial Assistant:	Stacy Wagner
Production Editor:	Julia Parnell
Copy Editor:	Kristin Bergstad
Proofreader:	Ruth Saavedra
Typesetter:	C&M Digitals (P) Ltd.
Cover Designer:	Tracy Miller
Graphic Designer:	Lisa Miller
Illustrations:	Tom Fisher
Photographs:	Samual Jones, III, & Patsy S. Queen

Contents

Foreword

The Frazzled Teacher is the prototype of the frazzled American professional. Teachers are a special group of people who have accepted their responsibilities to help ensure the education of America's future. This book can help you accomplish your work in the worst of situations and be more effective in the best of situations.

The Five Step Program for Reclaiming Time gives all teachers the tools to be as productive as your talents will allow you to be. The Queens have identified stress as a natural epidemic. Teacher burnout is an American tragedy, and if the combination of stress and teaching are inevitable, your succumbing to that stress need not be. Understanding your stress, predicting your most vulnerable times, and learning how to best cope, are acquired skills that take practice. This book can help you. This book can change you. Allen and Patsy have made an educated study of the stresses teachers face.

A majority of medical complaints can have their basis in stress. Physicians such as me deal with stress-induced symptoms on a regular basis and it is clear that stress can negatively affect your health. The authors discuss, in an insightful manner, the medical and psychological consequences of stress. Major points of healthy nutrition are outlined and exercise is put into a practical and fun format.

As experienced professionals, the Queens are direct, sometimes critical of the teaching profession and honest in their attempts to find answers for teachers working within an education system that includes rewards and sacrifices and disappointments. This book is preparatory for teachers-in-training, helpful to new teachers and a survival tool for seasoned veterans.

The Frazzled Teacher is a five step process that weaves you through what you need to know, do, and avoid. The book begins with defining the unique stressors associated with teaching school. Allen and Patsy walk you through how to prepare for, prevent, and deal with school-related stress. You will be taught to identify and separate the good from the bad types of stress. This is a critical concept to grasp and the Queens have it down. The authors go on to show how to better balance your personal and professional lives by focusing on managing priorities. As a result, you should be able to maintain a more healthy lifestyle, stay out of your doctor's office and be your most effective. Self-assessment tools, coping skills, and work book sections are included. Exercise is always a must for stress relief, and their approaches are innovative and varied. There is definitely something for everyone. Exercise comes alive in this book. In addition you will learn how to use your body and your mind for those times when immediate stress management is useful. Doing a good teaching job, without hurting yourself in the process, may be difficult if you are too much of a perfectionist or too much of a procrastinator. The Queens directly address these issues and give you options and time management strategies for all aspects of your work. They are quite frank in discussions about dealing with colleagues, superiors, and communication problems. The final section in this tutorial emphasizes the importance of balanced nutrition needed to be healthy and effective in life and in the classroom. Teachers need a lot of help in this arena and this section is all about habits, choices, snacks, and how to avoid temptations.

Donald Schumacher, M.D., Medical Director
Center for Nutrition and Preventative Medicine, PLLC
Charlotte, North Carolina
CNPMschum@aol.com

Note: Dr. Schumacher is nationally known as a medical researcher and practitioner, a leader in the medical community, well-published in the literature of nutrition and obesity, and has appeared on several national television programs including ABC 20/20 and ABC Primetime. Dr. Schumacher was recently appointed as Chairman of the Mecklenburg County Commissioners' Task Force for Healthy Weight in Children and Adolescents in Charlotte, North Carolina.

Acknowledgments

We would like to personally thank our editor, Faye Zucker, who inspired us to write this first book in a series on a topic that consumes so much of our life. Our appreciation goes to Kris Bergstad and to Julia Parnell for helping us to get this into production. Special thanks to Sam Jones, our photographer, and to Tom Fisher, who captured the essence in what we were trying to say in his wonderful cartoon drawings. In addition we would like to thank our models, who helped give a clear picture of some of the procedures to follow in the exercises—a special thanks to Judy.

The content comes from much experience in the classroom. We would like to thank our students, teachers and graduate assistants who shared ideas and information to further confirm what was needed to be included in the book.

Special thanks to Brian and Deana for your many hours of assistance.

And finally, we would like to thank Dr. Donald Shumacher for the great foreword to the book. To have someone of his caliber to endorse our work with such kind words is an honor we will treasure forever.

About the Authors

 **J. Allen Queen,** Ed.D., is currently Professor and Chair of the Department of Educational Leadership at The University of North Carolina at Charlotte and has been a classroom teacher, principal, college administrator and university professor. He has been a consultant to over 160 schools and districts in 36 states and 3 foreign countries in the areas of classroom discipline, school safety, block scheduling and time management.

Dr. Queen has written over 20 books and 70 articles including books on karate for children. He holds the rank of Godan, Fifth Degree Black Belt in Shito-ryu Karate and learned the art and science of stress management from this sport.

In addition to books, Allen has appeared on numerous radio and television programs, including *ABC World News Now*. Dr. Queen enjoys working with teachers and principals in the areas of managing priorities, time management and stress reduction. He has also worked with numerous universities, businesses, and government organizations in time and stress management. Allen was a major consultant for several years to the Justice Department in Washington as a presenter of the Attorney General's Selective Seminars.

Dr. Queen is an annual presenter at several national conferences and his favorite topic to present is Desktop Yoga.

Patsy S. Queen holds a B.S. Ed. and a B.S.N from Western Carolina University and a M.S.N. from the University of Texas at Austin. In addition to nursing care positions in North Carolina, Virginia and Texas, Patsy has twenty-five years experience in nursing education. Currently an instructor at Gaston College, she has taught classes in adult health, maternal-child health and nutrition. She has published articles in the *Journal of School Health* and the *Journal of Nursing Education* and is currently working on a project on nursing assessment of the newborn with Elsevier Publishing and the next book in the *Frazzled Series*. Patsy serves as an item writer for the National Council of State Boards of Nursing Registered Nurse (NCLEX-RN) Exam and the National Certification Corporation nursing specialty examination in Maternal-Infant Nursing. Patsy is recognized by the North Carolina Board of Nursing as a Clinical Specialist.

Rose and Blanche Queen are stress-reduction consultants for the Queen family. Research about the human-animal health connection can be found at www.deltasociety.org

Identifying Schools as a Culture of Stress

Figure 1.1 Teaching is a high-stress profession

A first-year teacher writes to her elementary methods professor:

Dear Dr. Smith:

Is my life supposed to be like this? Yesterday after teaching school all day I found myself running out the door as the custodian was locking the building to leave. Panic consumed me when I realized that I had spent the last hour comparing notes with colleagues to determine who has the most disruptive kids and, as a result, had left with tomorrow's lesson plans incomplete. As I carried two large boxes of instructional materials to my car, I could have been mistaken for an employee of a major moving van line.

Once I arrived home, I prepared dinner, washed the dishes, and put in a load of laundry. My husband got the twins their bath and then got them ready for bed. Sitting down to reflect upon the day's events, I wondered why I had to tell Marvin three times to put the crayons in the box. I felt guilty for losing my temper with three girls who continued to play after I gave clear directions for them to complete center work. I was close to a nervous breakdown as I wondered what miracle I must perform to get Jason to turn in his homework. It was getting late. I had a choice either to crash on the bed in total exhaustion; complete tomorrow's lesson plans; or read the want ads for a new job in the morning's paper that, by the way, was still unrolled. I crashed on the sofa before I could make the choice. Is this what teaching is all about?

Sincerely,

Jane Doe

SCHOOL CULTURE AND STRESS

Stress for today's teachers has become a national epidemic. Increased and continual anxiety to the degree that we experience has led to what has been labeled "teacher burnout." In fact, we believe that our nation's schools have become a "culture of stress." What is a culture of stress? A *culture* may be defined as a pattern of beliefs, values, and practices shared by a group or organization. Culture basically defines how things are done. *Stress,* clinically defined, is the sum of the biological reactions to any adverse stimulus, mental or emotional, internal or external, that tends to disturb the organism's balance. Today's teachers work in a *culture of stress* and are members of a profession that follows a pattern of expected practices that can disturb homeostasis.

In other words, as a teacher you can become sick teaching in a classroom or school environment that is stressful. And all classroom or school environments are stressful.

YOU HAVE TWO CHOICES

1. Use precautions or plan activities to prevent or eliminate the adverse stimuli, OR

2. If unpreventable (such as we experience daily in the classroom), you must counteract the adversity to reach life balance or return to a state of homeostasis.

Not Your Typical Jack and Jill Story

Jill knows that if she groups two boys known to fight with each other in a group activity, she will experience an adverse stimulus that will cause her stress. With this knowledge she uses precaution and planning and does not place them in the same group; therefore, she avoids the adverse stimulus and stress. On the other hand, Jack, totally unaware of this situation, groups the boys together and as expected they begin to fight. Jack experiences the adverse stimulus and the related stress. He becomes frustrated and moves the boys apart. His body is not in balance; biological reactions may include increased adrenaline, heart rate, and blood pressure. He is in an agitated state and is stressed. However, Jack has learned a special deep breathing exercise (one that you are going to learn in this book) and sits quietly for a few moments doing the quiet deep breathing activity and slowly returns his body to a state of homeostasis or what we call *life balance.*

Many health professionals use the term *distress* to differentiate between stress that is considered negative and stress that can be viewed as positive. However, even positive stress can cause problems if not balanced. Think of the holiday season, a wedding, or the birth of a child. The body really does not know the difference and attempts to return to the state of life balance as quickly as possible.

Though the term *stress* has become common in today's society, interpretations of the identity of stress vary greatly. Teacher burnout can be viewed as a state of physical, emotional, and mental exhaustion resulting from an inability to cope effectively with the daily stresses found in teaching over an extended period of time. The classroom teacher is a major candidate for burnout. Whether chasing twenty-five to thirty elementary children for six to seven hours or commanding 100 to 150 students for three ninety-minute or seven fifty-minute periods in a small space while attempting to teach, control behavior, reinforce, reward, socialize, and raise test scores, usually all at the same time, it does not take long for today's teacher to reach exhaustion.

> Unless you have been a teacher, you have no way to understand what we are saying. So, this book is for teachers, teacher assistants, parent volunteers . . .

Teaching Is a High-Stress Profession

Teaching is identified as a "high-stress" profession by researchers. Conflicting reports have surfaced, but 50% to 75% of teachers view teaching as a stressful job. Disenchantment can lead to teachers leaving the profession. Major sources of teacher stress today include:

- Unmotivated students,
- Discipline problems,
- Dealing with difficult school administrators, and
- Feeling unsafe in the school environment.

> Teaching is considered to be a high-stress profession.

Stress may be also defined as any situation in which one must adapt to change; and the demands of teaching change with the wind, creating an abundance of unchecked stress. In fact, more than 20% of teachers leave the profession within the first three years. And as new teachers enter America's schools over the next ten years, most will enter the ranks with enthusiasm, but the prediction is that 50% will leave the profession after five years and 80% after ten years.

Concerns from beginning teachers are remarkably similar to those of veteran teachers discussed above and may additionally include:

- Trying to cope with individual differences,
- Poor relationship with parents, and
- Lack of instructional organization.

It is our experience that a much greater number of today's teacher education graduates awarded teaching licensure or credentials do not go into teaching. Many are lured by businesses and industries promising higher salary and benefits, a healthier work environment, and lower levels of job stress. With this increased phenomenon and over one half of the teachers reaching retirement age within the next five to ten years, schools are experiencing a growing teacher shortage in about every level and subject area. School boards as a result are being forced to hire nonqualified individuals who are changing careers or rebounding from corporate and government downsizing. Once in the classroom, these new teachers soon discover the stigma that "anybody can teach" is a false and frightening claim. Unprepared to teach specific content areas or lacking basic teaching skills, most of these recruits are not willing to work through the early and largely overwhelming "hands-on" training program necessary to get them through the first year of teaching.

For More Information: Visit the following Web site for more information on teacher training: www.ncate.org (The National Council for Accreditation of Teacher Education).

Research Note

In the recent Kappan Gallup Poll (2002), 76% of the public respondents rated schools as seriously lacking student discipline. Seventy-three percent rated the problem of getting good teachers as a serious problem. In the same poll, 71% of the respondents believed the schools were seriously overcrowded and 63% believed the schools were seriously plagued with student fights, violence, and gangs. Working in schools with discipline problems, working when the public thinks we need to be better teachers, working in an over crowded and sometimes violent environment—who would not be stressed?

School Reform and Teacher Stress

The National Commission of Education intensified a long era of legislated school reform that enforced more rigorous teacher selection, teacher evaluation, standardization of curriculum, and testing of students.

The Perception

School reform has been predicated on the assumption that teachers are the problem or reason for mediocre school performance and therefore need to be carefully controlled and monitored. Educators are experiencing a time of "teacher bashing"—the wrongs of education and even society have been attributed to incompetent, inconsiderate, and self-serving teachers and administrators.

Since 1965, the Elementary and Secondary Education Act (ESEA) has provided the guidelines for the federal government's requirement for public schools. With the bipartisan support given to President George W. Bush in 2001, there now exists a redefined ESEA, often referred to as the No Child Left Behind Act. States must be in compliance with the national standards set forth by this legislation in order to receive federal monies, which requires more testing resulting in higher teacher and student stress in the classroom.

For More Information: To read more about No Child Left Behind visit: http://www.ed.gov/offices/OESE/esea and http://www.nochildleftbehind.gov/

Teaching and Non-Instructional Responsibilities

Handling discipline problems and receiving extra duties such as hall and cafeteria monitoring, among others, are viewed as detriments to teaching and are not considered a part of the "job description" by some teachers. Faculty meetings, homeroom duties, and high-stakes testing promote feelings of misusing valuable instructional time. Laws require the inclusion of students with various disabilities; special accommodations are therefore required of regular classroom teachers in order for these students to function at a minimum level, which just adds to the list of stressing concerns.

Students bring distracters and stressors—described as "life events"—to the classroom daily. Researchers designed and conducted a study that measured forty-two items using the Adolescent Life Events Checklist (ALEC). Condensing the forty-two items into sixteen subscales produced the following list:

1. Change in eating and sleeping habits
2. Death or accident of friend or relative
3. Problems with friends
4. Sexual events (pregnancy, abortion, miscarriage)
5. Change in status of parents
6. Family conflict
7. Satanism or magic
8. Substance-use issues of self or family member
9. Mother's pregnancy or miscarriage
10. Problems with police
11. Delinquent activities
12. Money and employment problems of self or family member
13. Physical violence

14. School stressors

15. Personal injury or illness

16. Sexual abuse

Research Note

Frequency of the occurrence of the life events was examined by the researchers to determine which events occurred to more than half the student participants in the individual schools involved in the study. Three life events appeared in the top six for all schools involved: "death of close friend or relative," "money problems experienced by the family," and "change in relationship with people you know." When students are stressed and upset, their behavior usually deteriorates and teacher stress levels can increase proportionally.

Problems that many students bring to the classroom as "social baggage" lead to additional stress on teachers. Teachers cannot and should not be required to deal with family problems, street life, or community problems, but often the teacher, especially the elementary teacher, has to serve in multiple roles ranging from nurse to counselor. These extra duties or expectations add to the level of stress.

WARNING: Prolonged exposure to high levels of stress without effective coping leads to health problems. Stress and related anxiety can manifest in a plethora of physical problems: tachycardia (racing heart), high blood pressure, asthma, abdominal pains, headaches, backaches, and other somatic complaints.

TEACHER STRESS AND THE IMMUNE SYSTEM

Stress affects the immune system of our bodies. A high percentage of teachers express job dissatisfaction. Dissatisfaction over a long period of limited control or inability to change can lead to distress and health problems.

Researchers studying psychoneuroimmunology (PNI) have scientifically proven domains of stress affect the immune system. Evidence showed stress might cause a measurable decline in the immune system's ability to fight disease. Over the years, theoretical explanations have emerged grounded in scientific study. Medical findings appear to imply anyone experiencing stress can have a decrease in immune function.

Defense against infectious disease is controlled by the immune system. Foreign substances that are not naturally part of the body are attacked by the immune system.

Not confined to one organ or one site in the body, the immune system is everywhere. Immune cells occupy the skin, eyes, nostrils, lungs, and the lining of internal organs. Every part of the body is occupied. In different ways, an assortment of specialized cells protects the body. When a part of the body gives a distress call, immune cells charge to the problem area via the lymphatic system.

> To learn more about the technical aspects of lymphocytes, T-cells, and NK-cells, visit www.webdoctor.com

Possible Consequences of Stress

Stress has the potential to depress immunity. This may be one of the reasons why people under stress are more susceptible to illness. Hormonal deregulation caused by stressful events leads to inflammatory disease and depression. Stress affects immune responses to viruses and bacteria. Therefore it is believed that chronic stress increases susceptibility to the common cold.

> ### Research Note
> High levels of cortisol, a stress hormone found in the bloodstream, affect immune function. If these levels remain high for too long, individuals may suffer related illnesses, including winter colds and flu.

Stress may lessen the effectiveness of certain vaccines and can confound some studies of certain illnesses such as AIDS and autoimmune diseases. Vaccinations for hepatitis B and for influenza were influenced by stress, causing a suppression of T-cell response and lowering antibody levels. These are two factors imperative for developing a strong immunity to these diseases.

Researchers from the University of California-Los Angeles examined the relationship between stressful life events and the development of colorectal cancer. Men under stress were five times more likely to get colorectal cancer than men without job difficulties.

A profound stressor is job dissatisfaction. For many reasons previously discussed, teachers have been dissatisfied with their job. One reason may be that educators encounter continual daily conflicts that are persistent and repetitive and go unchecked. Individually these events may not pose much harm, but collectively this accumulated stressor can become problematic. Teachers receive stressors from internal, external, and personal pressures. When individuals feel demands from the environment and these demands cannot be handled appropriately, stress occurs.

> A combination of teaching and personal pressures makes stress the #1 health problem of classroom teachers.

TEACHING AND PERSONALIZING STRESS

Internal and External Stressors

Internal pressures trigger stress in teachers. Internal stressors may include: isolation from other adults and dealing with the unique learning abilities and weaknesses of individual students. Other internal stressors consist of deadlines, bells, excessive paper work, inadequate supplies, preparation, and grading. Teachers may also feel internal stressors from being harassed or questioned by students. Students tend to complain verbally about assignments and may physically damage personal property in the classroom. Student absenteeism can also be stressful because it requires additional work by the teacher. Each stressor not only affects the teacher's health, but instructional class time as well.

External pressures are additional stressors teachers deal with daily. Such stressors include: dealing with parents, working with mentors or supervisors, and interacting with administrators. Violence at school is another external stressful situation. Circumstances surrounding violence are time-consuming and require paperwork. Each stressor uses individuals' energy and may cause stress hormones to activate.

An educator's personal stress may also affect immunity. Personal stressors include: death of a loved one, car accident, illness of a family member, divorce, debt, trouble with in-laws, changes in living conditions, and financial situations. Even though personal stressors were not caused at school, each stressor may affect a teacher's classroom performance. Personal stress may contribute to additional internal and external pressures during an educator's day.

Research Note

Harvard physiologist Walter B. Cannon first described the fight-or-flight response. In this response the body reacts internally to a threat. Acute stress could be dealt with effectively by either fighting or running away. This response was essential to survival when human beings faced physical threats such as wild animals. However, in modern life the stresses we face are more likely psychological and inter-personal. A stress researcher at McGill University concluded that the body reacts to today's stresses as though it were still facing an actual physical threat. Stressful situations have always caused the body to react.

Responding to Stress

Individuals encounter three basic stages in response to stress.

- Stage 1, alarm, refers to the body mobilizing for "fighting or fleeing."
- Stage 2, resistance, is where the individual combats the stressor. Through purposeful action, the individual attempts to reduce the stressor by using coping tactics.
- Stage 3, exhaustion, is referred to as burnout.

Each of the above three stages can be compared to diving into cold water. First the body is "alarmed" by the frigid water. Second, the body is able to swim for a period of time while it builds up "resistance" to the cold. Finally, the swimmer becomes "exhausted" if the water is too cold or the swimming too long. In response to stress, each individual stage affects the function of the immune system.

Aspects of immune function may be bolstered by bursts of short-term stress. When stressful situations become chronic, however, the immune system may falter and health problems arise. Physiologically the body reacts each time a stressor is present. In response to Stage 1, "fighting or fleeing," the immune system causes changes to occur within the body. First, adrenaline starts to pour throughout the body and affects immune functions. An individual's heart rate begins to accelerate. Then an increase in blood pressure and blood clotting occurs. Whereas most functions speed up in stressful situations, the digestive system slows down. If a teacher continually encounters stressful experiences, severe physiological symptoms may begin to occur. Such symptoms include: insomnia, upset stomach, ulcers, ulcerative colitis, headaches, migraines, chronic back pain, asthma, fainting, fever, diabetes, stuttering, skin rashes, menstrual problems, Graves' disease, hypoglycemia, multiple sclerosis, arteriosclerosis, arthritis, anxiety, and depression.

Physiological disorders can affect the work completed by teachers. For instance, educators may plan less often or less carefully, teachers may teach class less enthusiastically and creatively, and they may stay home from work more often. Furthermore, educators may feel less sympathetic toward students and less optimistic about the future. Teachers may also get frustrated more easily by classroom disturbances and become irritated by a lack of student progress.

Stress reactions tend to follow a stage-by-stage process. Frustration is frequently the first reaction, and causes a wide range of feelings from irritation to anger.

High levels of anxiety may be created by increased demands or a greater degree of role uncertainty. A teacher's ability to make decisions may be unproductive because ability to concentrate is reduced. Teachers may experience a feeling of panic or a sharp loss of confidence in teaching ability. When there is prolonged exposure to a situation that causes anxiety, teachers may reach the exhaustion threshold. Feelings of tiredness are often described as "feeling 'drained.'"

There is a risk that teachers will become burned out if exhaustion levels are not relieved. Teachers who are burned out are completely drained emotionally, physically, behaviorally, mentally, sexually, and spiritually. Acute stress transforms into chronic stress once a teacher reaches the burnout stage.

The Dangers of Teacher Burnout

Educators experience stress in different ways and for different reasons. Continuation of stressful situations causes the immune system to undergo system disorder. In general, teachers who encounter stress are usually irritable, anxious, angry, or sad. However, chronic stress may lead to severe problems throughout the body.

Read Closely

Negative stress from psychological, cardiovascular, respiratory, and physical traumas has proven to affect teachers' health. The immune system's connection to bodily systems results in a significant correlation between stress and health. Psychological and somatic complaints by teachers include: fatigue and weakness, blurred vision, irritability, sensitivity to weather, dizziness, malaise, and depression. Dysfunctional cardiovascular systems have affected educators through palpitations, hypertension, arteriosclerosis, and coronary

(Continued)

(Continued)

artery disease. Musculoskeletal problems manifest as back difficulties, cervical tension, and headaches. Respiratory system dysfunctions have caused repeated upper respiratory infections, bronchial problems, asthma, and hyperventilation. Lastly, physical trauma may include: lacerations, bruises, head injuries, seizures, and deafness.

Chronic stress may lead to severe problems throughout the body.

Research Note

Studies have shown teachers who tend to be unhappy, measured by psychological testing, were more likely to have recurrent cold sores. Higher levels of antibodies to herpes viruses were common in people under various kinds of stress. High levels of antibodies to herpes indicate low immune function. Consistent and convincing evidence proves stress can affect the body's control over herpes virus infections.

Autoimmune disease stems from excessive immune system activity. Rheumatoid arthritis, systemic lupus erythematosus (SLE), and Type 1 diabetes are included in these diseases. In autoimmune diseases, antibodies mistakenly identify the body's healthy cells as foreign invaders and attack. Life-threatening organ damage and chronic inflammation are the result. Acute stress activates the immune system, and stress precipitates these illnesses.

More than 50% of urban high school teachers—41% in New York, 53% in Chicago, and 77% in San Diego—reported that their work has caused them physical illness.

Nationally, teacher absenteeism has nearly doubled in the public schools in the past twenty years.

MANAGING SCHOOL STRESSORS

Refocusing on Teacher Roles

Teachers should not feel alone when managing their stress in the classroom. School leaders can do several things to help manage teacher stress. The first of these is to specify and clarify prescribed roles and expectations and ensure that teachers are given the roles in which they can operate most effectively. This could mean that principals ensure that the workload is spread appropriately and individual teachers are not overloaded.

In addition, the authors believe that support plays an important role in stress reduction:

- Working in a school where there is social support is important. Social support enables teachers to share concerns with each other, which can lead to helpful suggestions from colleagues that teachers can implement in order to help resolve the sources of stress.
- Participation of all staff in staff development programs can lead to professional socialization.
- Simply sharing problems or engaging in some social activity with colleagues can often effectively help dissipate the feelings of stress.
- Also, since teachers themselves reduce stress through physical exercise and interpersonal communication, schools and districts may benefit from developing programs and activities within their buildings that promote regular physical exercise and opportunities for staff dialogue and social support.

Principals Can Help

Principals need to think about how administrative actions create unnecessary sources of stress. For example, a principal can set unrealistic deadlines for the completion of certain tasks or fail to communicate adequately with others, which then gives rise to avoidable problems. Principals can provide support to help teachers relieve frustration that can raise anxiety levels. We have found two areas on which principals should focus to manage teacher stress. The first is to help teachers manage reactions to stress. For example, principals can bring relaxation training, health and wellness programs, and time management seminars to their schools. The second is to assist teachers in establishing clear guidelines and responsibilities by seeking teacher input in goal setting and decision making, providing social support time for teachers, and developing the setting for superior mentor relationships. Teachers can make great partners. Principals and teachers can work together to reduce stress at school and in the classroom.

> Develop and use a schoolwide classroom and discipline plan such as *Positive Discipline* by Nelson or *Responsible Discipline* by Queen. For more information on classroom discipline, visit www.responsiblediscipline.com

TWENTY-ONE PLANNING TECHNIQUES TO PREVENT CLASSROOM STRESS

Listed below are twenty-one ideas shared by teachers throughout the nation. Teachers, principals, and school administrators can use these techniques throughout their schools to reduce classroom stress.

1. Develop and use a schoolwide classroom management plan
2. Acknowledge individuals with sincere statements of appreciation
3. Establish common planning time for departments, teams, or grade levels
4. Schedule occasional duty-free lunch periods
5. Organize first-year teachers' support group
6. Have mentors available on same grade levels or content area
7. Limit faculty meetings to once per month
8. Minimize classroom interruptions of all types
9. Keep communication open with school administrators
10. Develop a teacher buddy system for networking and support

11. Use newsletters and notice boards for sharing information instead of more meetings

12. Plan workday social activities for morale building

13. Ban negative talk in the teachers' lounge

14. Allow freedom of lesson plan format

15. Plan teacher-recognition activities

16. Have upper grade students provide assistance in clerical duties

17. Keep instructional resources cataloged by grade level or subject area

18. Provide meaningful staff development for practical use in the classroom

19. Provide greater support from principals with parent-related issues

20. Acquire advanced technology, training, and support for record keeping

21. Implement flexible scheduling to improve effective use of classroom instruction.

For More Information: Visit the following Web site on scheduling and improved classroom instruction: www.blockscheduling.com

Restructuring Personal and Teaching Priorities for a Healthy Lifestyle

Figure 2.1 Do you know what your *real* priorities are?

WHY MANAGE PRIORITIES?

Assume that some major catastrophe has just occurred or is in process. It may be your house on fire, an automobile accident, or a plane crash. In thirty seconds write down three things that come immediately to mind:

1. _make sure everyone escaped safely_
2. _call for help_
3. _keep everyone together and calm_

Probably, if you are honest with yourself, most of the items that you listed are related to your spouse or significant other, children, family members or friends, and perhaps spiritual or deeply personal thoughts. As you may have heard before, people who are terminally ill do not think about the things left undone at work or related professional concerns. However, if you are like most teachers, you are constantly thinking about lesson plans, problem students, and papers needing to be graded. It is truly amazing how we can change our thought patterns when serious situations occur. In actuality, most of the items you listed are really THE REAL priorities in your life. Yet due to lack of time, to stress, and the ability to do the wrong things well, THE REAL priorities may have been neglected. Think about it!

Managing priorities can be a difficult task for you to accomplish. Often, as you can see in the first activity, little time may be given to the *real* priorities in your life. Why manage priorities?

> Simple—to give you *more time* to do the things *you want to do and to lower your stress level.* You manage priorities to give yourself more PERSONAL time to do the things that YOU want to do.

Bob and Jane: Sound Familiar?

Bob, a biology teacher, loves to sail. However, due to conflicting schedules, he never seems to find the time. Even when he does get to sail, he finds his thoughts returning to

(Continued)

(Continued)

tasks left incomplete on his desk at school. Bob is suffering from *priority guilt.* He is preoccupied with thoughts of his teaching responsibilities and becomes anxiety ridden and stressed, thus failing to enjoy his sailing trip.

Jane, a new department chair in the English department, is thrilled about her new position, but she soon discovers that the hours she has always reserved just for herself for reading, walking, and other relaxing activities that she enjoys are now gone. She notices an increase in her anxiety level and faces the demands of her new job in a less than positive manner.

As teachers, Bob and Jane are putting more of their personal time and energy into their teaching priorities. These priorities are in constant competition with their personal priorities. We all have teaching priorities and personal priorities that in many instances may be in continuous competition.

In the next activity, your goal is to set up a program that will allow you to begin to set a balance between professional and personal priorities.

Set a Balance Between Professional and Personal Priorities

You begin determining priorities—both professionally and personally—by identifying problem areas. If you are unable to determine your problems, you will often solve the wrong problems (see Figure 2.2).

Figure 2.2 Identifying Your Priority Areas: Problem Analysis I

In completing the following activity, examine each item and rate your perception by completing the sentence with *Usually* (mark with the letter A), *Sometimes* (mark with the letter B), or *Seldom* (mark with the letter C). We strongly recommend that you have a close family member and a professional colleague rate you in the same areas so you can compare their perceptions with yours. The closer their ratings are to yours, the better your assessment of what is really happening in your life.

(Continued)

Figure 2.2 (Continued)

Be sure to ask individuals who will be honest and fair to you in their ratings.

Example: From my perception, I	*Usually*	*Sometimes*	*Seldom*
1. Have enough time for myself.		B	

From my perception, I	*Usually*	*Sometimes*	*Seldom*
1. Have enough time for myself.		*B*	
2. Have enough time for my family.		*B*	
3. Have enough time for responsibilities at school.	*A*		
4. Have a clear understanding of ALL my priorities.		*B*	
5. Set long-range and short-range goals.	*A*		
6. Achieve my teaching goals.	*A*		
7. Maintain a high level of energy.		*B*	
8. Maintain a high level of enthusiasm.		*B*	
9. Am motivated to do my best in teaching.	*A*		
10. Avoid postponing difficult or unpleasant tasks.	*A*		
11. Consolidate activities at home.	*A*		
12. Keep a place for everything.		*B*	
13. Manage change effectively, personally, and professionally		*B*	
14. Can say "no" easily and tactfully, even to my principal.			*C*
15. Use time wisely in the classroom and personally.	*A*		
16. Allow other people to use their time appropriately.		*B*	

Figure 2.2 (Continued)

17. Control interruptions to my
    planned lessons. _____ *B* _____

18. Avoid taking on too many
    responsibilities, especially
    at school. _____ *B* _____

19. Avoid taking on too many
    responsibilities with my
    family/friends. _____ *B* _____

20. Coordinate work with others. _____ *B* _____

21. Delegate responsibilities
    responsibly to family members. _____ _____ *C*

22. Communicate well with
    colleagues and administrators. *A* _____ _____

23. Listen while others talk,
    especially students. *A* _____ _____

24. Maintain a high level of
    written communication skills. _____ *B* _____

25. Manage totally unexpected
    change effectively. *A* _____ _____

26. Manage well in crisis situations
    at home and school. *A* _____ _____

27. Prioritize my personal interests. _____ *B* _____

28. Review personal goals
    periodically. _____ *B* _____

29. Keep a personal daily, weekly,
    monthly, and yearly plan. _____ _____ *C*

30. Acknowledge personal and
    teaching weaknesses. _____ *B* _____

You may notice that statements are included from both personal and teaching situations. Re-examine the thirty items. For any item that you marked with a C (*Seldom*), identify that problem on the following page as personal, teaching, or both.

(Continued)

Figure 2.2 (Continued)

Areas for You to Examine Further

Problem Analysis 1 for Personal Priorities

1. _21_
2. _29_
3. _____
4. _____
5. _____

Problem Analysis 1 for Teaching Priorities

1. _14_
2. _21_
3. _____
4. _____
5. _____

Next, examine each column closely.

1. Do you see any item that is listed in both professional and personal?

2. How do your ratings compare with those of your family member or colleague?

3. Analyze which of these items under Personal and Teaching causes you the most frustration. As previously stated, it is important to see how family and colleagues may have rated you (if you chose to include that in this activity), but it is now time for just YOU to further analyze both columns for which items cause you the most frustration or stress, and to organize these in *priority* order with the most frustrating being number 1.

My Priority Order of Frustrations and Stress

Personal

1. _21_
2. _29_

3. _____

4. _____

5. _____

Teaching

1. _14_

2. _21_

3. _____

4. _____

5. _____

Eric: Profile of a New Teacher

Eric is new to teaching. He had been in the business world for almost twenty years before his company downsized and he lost his job. He and his wife have two teenage children at home, and he decides to try teaching. Entering as a lateral-entry teacher while working on his teaching certificate, Eric soon experiences many stressful situations. As his duties increase, he notices dramatic increases in stress and frustration. In addition, the children have gotten older and their social lives have taken larger amounts of time away from home and family responsibilities. Eric, however, not wanting to cause friction at his new job or at home, fails to be assertive and assumes greater numbers of tasks and responsibilities. When Eric completed the activity in Figure 2.2, he realized that he had a problem with Items 2, 3, 8, 10, 11, 18, 19, 20, and 30 in his personal and teaching lives. First he recorded the responses that he felt were important for him to address. His next step was to list, *in order of priority*, the areas in which he saw the most frustrating or stressful problems.

Eric's Problem Analysis

Personal Analysis 1

Eric made a list of the items in his personal life:

1. Avoid taking on too many responsibilities with my family/ friends (Item 19)

2. Have enough time for my family (Item 2)

3. Consolidate activities at home (Item 11)

4. Avoid postponing difficult or unpleasant tasks (Item 10)

5. Coordinate work with others (Item 20)

Teaching Analysis 1

Eric made a list of the items in his teaching life:

1. Acknowledge personal and teaching weaknesses (Item 30)

2. Avoid taking on too many responsibilities, especially at school (Item 18)

3. Avoid postponing difficult or unpleasant tasks (Item 10)

4. Have enough time for responsibilities at school (Item 3)

5. Maintain a high level of enthusiasm (Item 8)

As can be observed, Eric had many of the same issues in both lists, but in a different priority. As you completed Problem Analysis I you may have discovered a similar pattern or a totally different one. The important task is to determine your needs. If you have less than ten areas, super; but try not to list more than five items in each area.

A MIRROR IMAGE OF SELF

Once you have determined your basic need areas, it is time for a closer examination of self. Five major components combine to make up "A Mirror Image of Self." These areas are physical, emotional, intellectual, professional, and social. Every event, item, or activity in your life is related to one or more of these areas. You should be aware that millions of individuals pay exorbitant amounts of money annually to determine problem areas. Of course, nothing replaces getting a complete physical examination, but probably you are aware if you are physically fit. In addition, you know your basic intelligence level, your sociability, and your emotional stability. Problem Analysis II is a fun, but important, activity to determine problems and begin a plan for improvement.

Meet Susan, An Elementary Teacher

Susan, an elementary teacher, has entered into her late twenties. In college she was trim, energetic, and healthy. As her duties and responsibilities at school increased so did her eating habits. In addition to carrying thirty pounds of extra weight, she seldom exercised. She felt depressed because the offers for an evening out were less than she received ten years ago. Her afternoons and evenings were filled with additional time at school with few social outlets. Once a voracious reader, Susan did not have the energy or take the time to venture into new books or intellectual activities. As Susan sat down to complete "The Mirror Image of Self," she was shocked into the realization that the problems had gotten out of hand. Her analysis was as follows:

Physically

I am 30 pounds overweight and out of shape.

I can lose the excess weight and get in shape.

I need to get a physical and begin a diet and exercise program.

I will make the appointment for the physical examination immediately and begin the recommended diet and exercise programs as supervised.

Emotionally

I am finding myself smiling less these days.

(Continued)

(Continued)

I can smile more.

I need to smile more and view things positively.

I will purchase a self-help book or see a professional for help.

Intellectually

I am of above-average intelligence.

I can discuss numerous topics.

I need to read more often.

I will visit the library once a week.

Professionally

I am a competent and effective teacher.

I can deal with my class, which has several major discipline problems.

I need to find an effective way to manage my class and to lower my stress level.

I will effectively manage my class and lower my stress level at school.

Socially

I am growing more and more unsociable.

I can see myself becoming more distant from my friends.

I need to be more sociable, open, and relaxed.

I will find a method to relax so I can become more sociable.

By being honest and conducting an informal analysis of herself, Susan was ready to begin the process of improvement. She now knows her problem areas. Now it is time for you to complete the activity analysis in the five areas. Nobody else has to see your evaluation. This is for your improvement—so be honest and direct.

Figure 2.3   Your Mirror Image of Self: Problem Analysis II

Complete the following statements.

Physically . . .
I am *in pretty good shape*
I can *stand to lose 10 - 15 pounds*
I need *to eat healthier*
I will *journal my food intake & exercise*

Emotionally . . . *stressed about children / unhappy*
I am *struggling w/ personal relationships*
I can *approach / learn to let go*
I need *to let my grown children solve their own pblm*
I will *only get involved when asked*

Intellectually . . .
I am *intelligent*
I can *discuss a variety of topics intelligently*
I need
I will

Professionally . . .
I am *good at my job*
I can *always find ways to improve*
I need *to be more creative with lessons*
I will *find sources for innovative lessons*

Socially . . .
I am *struggling w/ friendships*
I can *reach out to others*
I need *friends I can turn to for support / give & take*
I will *call my friends more often / get together*

Managing Personal and Teaching Priorities

Thus far you have examined the concept of managing priorities and have analyzed some problems you face personally and in teaching. To be an effective teacher, you must know how

Figure 2.4 Managing Priorities

Examine and respond to the following:

1. How can your personal life influence your teaching?

Having a controlling-type personality with my family may not allow me the comfort level to let my children be creative and self sufficient.

2. To be the best teacher I can be, I must:

A. *not control or direct creativity as much*

B. *allow students to make mistakes*

C. *create more self-directed activities.*

D.

E.

to manage priorities with your students, colleagues, family, and for YOU.

In Question 1, you may have responded by stating that it is difficult to completely separate personal and professional personalities. Usually if you are a demanding, driving, high-expectations type of person in your personal life, you will have a similar style of managing or working with students and colleagues. Conversely, if you are unorganized, careless, or unconcerned personally, you probably will have a similar attitude professionally.

In Question 2, if you listed such qualities as highly competent, dedicated, well-planned, energetic, flexible, authentic, fair, and the like, you are on target with the attributes for being an excellent teacher.

Now that you have determined your priorities, it is time to examine methods you can use to find the APPROPRIATE time for implementing your priorities and METHODS to better manage stress in your life.

Mastering the Science of Stress Management for Better Health

Figure 3.1 Physical exercise is an effective form of stress
management

(handwritten marginalia: direct. making … a change … the source of stress … palliative … how we cope mentally and physically … eliminate)

MANAGING YOUR STRESS

Teachers can do many things to manage and reduce stress. Individual coping strategies fall into two main categories: direct action techniques and palliative techniques.

Individuals can use direct action techniques to eliminate the source of stress by first getting a clear idea as to the source. They then carry out some form of action that will deal successfully with the source of stress in the future by changing the situation in some way so that the scenario no longer occurs. Direct action techniques involve managing or organizing oneself more effectively. Direct action also involves developing new knowledge, skills, and work practices. Finally, direct action may be as simple as negotiating with colleagues, so that a teacher's situation is changed or dealt with by others.

Kyriacou recently reported that palliative techniques are techniques that lessen the feeling of stress that occurs. Palliative mental strategies involve the teacher's trying to change how the situation is appraised. Palliative physical strategies involve activities that help the teacher regain a sense of being relaxed by relieving any tension and anxiety that has built up.

We believe an individual's locus of control influences the relationship between work-related sources of stress and mental well-being. That is, individuals with an internal locus of control will be more likely to use direct action strategies that focus on altering the stressful situation. In contrast, individuals who perceive the causes of stress to be external may adopt palliative coping strategies. Some might argue that these "internals" direct their coping efforts to a more limited number of strategies than do "externals." And teachers are no different!

Most of us have discovered that personal coping strategies suggest that the most successful actions are those that are deemed positive—cognitive strategies, including positive thinking, setting realistic expectations, pragmatism, and blocking the negative all can help the individual teacher cope with stress.

Other examples of the positive management of stress include physical strategies, some of which are active (recreation, sports, and general exercise) and others more passive (listening to music, watching TV, reading). All of these can help the teacher manage stress.

> *The authors believe that the most effective form of stress management is physical exercise.*

We believe the most effective form of stress management is physical exercise. Furthermore, individuals need to learn both how to find physical outlets for stress and to distance themselves from their jobs. We have learned that practicing any routine that requires little thought—like walking the dog, doing housework, and mowing the lawn—can help an individual manage stress. The ideas listed below may also be helpful in managing stress.

- Keep problems in a realistic perspective.
- Avoid confrontations whenever possible.
- Try to relax before, during, and after work.
- Become a problem solver and work as part of a team.
- Express your feelings to others and be honest.
- Create a healthy lifestyle.
- Prioritize and keep your priorities in sight.
- Learn and remember your own limitations.

These strategies highlight the importance of teachers' recognizing their own perception of the degree of stress being experienced, and that individual action and successful coping can create a positive cycle whereby the same "objective" situation can be less demanding. More easily said than done!

In Box 3.1, perhaps you'll complete the first statement by adding one word such as "painful," "frustrating," or "necessary." You may elaborate with a more detailed statement such as, "Stress is manageable." In the second sentence you may have concluded that when you are stressed, you feel "anxious" or "upset."

Box 3.1

YOUR PERSONAL STRESS LEVEL

Take a few seconds to complete the following statements:

1. Stress is *uncomfortable but avoidable*

---

2. When I am stressed, I feel *pressured.*
I feel out of control of the situation

STRESS OCCURS WHEN YOUR BODY REACTS TO CHANGE.

These changes can be physical, mental, or emotional and can be positive or negative. For example, stress can be a result of positive changes that can occur when you buy a new house, receive a job promotion, or have a child. In contrast, stress can be a result of negative changes in your life such as the death of a loved one, uncertainty about priorities, or the presence of financial difficulties.

The results of positive stress and negative stress are different. The difference appears to be in the way your body *reacts or adapts* to the positive or negative changes that determine your stress level. For instance, you receive a job promotion. Although you are excited about the promotion, the changes that it brings, such as more responsibility or higher expectations from your boss, can cause stress. If you view this change as positive, your body will accept or adapt to the change, thereby limiting or decreasing the problems that are associated with the stress. Another example: You are fired from your job. Your body reacts to this change as negative. You feel defeated or alienated. You may be angry. Concerns of financial insecurity and possible loss of personal property begin to surface. When this occurs the effects of stress can be devastating.

The cumulative effects of continued stress or failure of your body to *accept or adapt* to change over a long period of time can bring about health problems such as the following:

- Headaches
- Impotence
- Ulcers
- Depression
- Back pain
- Weight loss or gain
- Dizziness
- Insomnia

In addition, many health professionals associate high blood pressure, cancer, and heart disease with uncontrolled stress. It is important to note that your negative stress can become positive stress and vice versa. Just as you can turn the loss of a job into a promotion by moving to a better company or starting your own successful business, your inability to adapt to the pressure or expectations of a promotion, once viewed as positive, can become negative and quite stressful.

Sources of stress, whether major or minor, can be labeled as internally or externally produced. External events such as traffic jams, long unscheduled meetings, and increased paperwork can create a physical or mental change that is stressful. Internal stress brought about by anger, frustration, or guilt can be equally as stressful. From one perspective you can sense that before external events become stressful, you have to internalize the event. For example, you are in a thirty-minute traffic jam. If this external event over which you have limited control causes you frustration (internal event), you will experience stress. On the other hand, if you sit quietly and listen to the radio, dictate a letter, or read an article until the traffic starts to move again, you feel productive and not stressed. Be sure not to read or talk on the telephone while you are actually driving.

As you can see, the way you view the situation or the way your body reacts and adapts to external events can limit your internal stress level. Of course, this is personal—individuals react differently to external and internal stress.

Stress and Temperament

In addition to high levels of unchecked stress being associated with physical illnesses, stress can influence your temperament, moods, and behavior. Think of your present employment situation. Maybe you have received an additional assignment. Time is short and you lack the appropriate resources. However, you strive to complete the project on time with a maximum degree of success. After leaving school, your car will not start. Frustrated, you feel your stress level rise. By the time you get your car started or repaired and you arrive home, you may not be in the best of moods or be pleasant with your spouse or children. If you have a confrontation with a family member at this time, you are more susceptible to being short or snappy, maybe even hostile.

Stress capacity is the amount of stress an individual can absorb before a negative reaction occurs.

Of course, you are aware that everyone has experienced similar situations and that stressful reactions are normal. The problem appears to be related to the individual's "stress capacity" or the amount of stress an individual can absorb before a negative reaction occurs. As in the situation above, you may have handled your stress level with ease—maybe even laughed the mishaps off. Your colleague in the same situation may have become ill, kicked the dog, or driven to the closest bar. At any particular time, in any particular problem or family situation, individuals can and will react differently.

It is impossible to list all of the factors that influence your stress level. Obviously, factors like personality, personal/professional security, self-concept, physical condition, genetics, past successes or failures, relevance, attitude, and sleeping and eating patterns (the list is endless) will determine your ability to handle stress. Every individual is different. In fact, individual stress levels can change or be affected by frequency of problems or intensity of problems, as in the "final straw" concept.

As you know, most things in moderation may not cause major problems. Even an intense, stressful situation can have minor or limited negative influence on you, especially if you recover in a reasonable time. The body has amazing recuperative abilities.

However, if your intensity remains high and frequency increases, your stress capacity will be overcharged and problems can result. The damage from stress appears to occur when one's stress capacity is exceeded. The longer it is exceeded, the greater the damage.

As previously stated, numerous physical ailments can be related to intense and frequent stress. Of great interest is a situation, usually prior to physical or mental problems developing, causing a change in your temperament. This can be *one* of your major indicators for checking your present stress capacity and determining if you need to make changes in your life to lower stress.

Questionnaire A.   Your Personal Stress Level

Take a few moments to answer the following personal questions with a yes or no.

1. In the past two months, has a family member told you that you appeared "uptight," "stressed out," or "tired"?

   Yes _____ No __✓__

2. In the past two months has a friend told you that you appeared "uptight," "stressed out," or "tired"?

   Yes __✓__ No _____

3. In the past two months have more than three individuals told you that you appeared "uptight," "stressed out," or "tired"?

   Yes _____ No __✓__

4. Do you find yourself more argumentative, snappy, or "short" with family or friends?

   Yes _____ No __✓__

5. Do friends or family members appear shocked, surprised, or become emotional with your actions or reactions to events, problems, conversations, and so on?

   Yes _____ No __✓__

6. If the answer to Question 5 is yes, is this more than they did two months ago?

    Yes _____ No _____

7. Do you feel you have surpassed your stress capacity or your ability to handle stress?

    Yes _____ No _✓_

8. Do you feel depressed, anxious or stressed?

    Yes _✓_ No _____

9. Do you drink alcohol to relax?

    Yes _____ No _✓_

10. If you answered yes to Question 9, has your alcohol consumption increased in the past two months?

    Yes _____ No _____

Note the answers in which you responded by checking *yes*. Add up the points for your *yes* answers. Only *yes* answers are counted.

1. Yes = 2 points	6. Yes = 2 points
2. Yes = 2 points	7. Yes = 2 points
3. Yes = 2 points	8. Yes = 2 points
4. Yes = 2 points	9. Yes = 2 points
5. Yes = 2 points	10. Yes = 2 points

Your total: _4_

Based on scores by teachers completing this survey, if your score was 0–4, you probably have no major stress problem with relationship to temperament changes. If you scored 6–14, there may be lifestyle issues (stress or other factors) you need to examine further. If you scored above 14 points, you may be in need of professional assistance.

Questionnaire B.   Your Professional Stress Level

Complete the following *professional* questions by checking *yes* or *no*.

1. In the past two months, have colleagues, students, or administrators stated that you looked tired or appeared stressed?

    Yes __✓__ No _____

2. In the past two months, have more than three individuals stated that you looked tired or appeared stressed?

    Yes _____ No _✓_

3. Have you received additional duties at work that require more time, detail, and responsibility?

    Yes _____ No _✓_

4. Do you feel that you have a time management problem at school?

    Yes _____ No _✓_

5. Do you find yourself daydreaming or romanticizing about times that were not as demanding or that required less time and gave you more freedom?

    Yes _✓_ No _____

6. If the answer to Question 5 is yes, is this more frequent than two months ago?

    Yes _____ No _✓_

7. Do you exceed 60 hours per week in teaching, planning, and grading activities?

    Yes _____ No _✓_

8. Do you prefer not to be bothered by people while at school, especially before and after school?

    Yes _____ No _✓_

9. Do you feel more depressed, anxious, or stressed when at school?

   Yes _____ No _✓_

10. Do you take anti-anxiety medication before or during school hours?

   Yes _____ No _✓_

Look at the questions to which you responded by checking *yes*. Add up the points to your *yes* answers. Only *yes* answers are counted.

1. Yes = 2 points	6. Yes = 2 points
2. Yes = 2 points	7. Yes = 2 points
3. Yes = 2 points	8. Yes = 2 points
4. Yes = 2 points	9. Yes = 2 points
5. Yes = 2 points	10. Yes = 2 points

Your total: _4_

Based on norms from teachers completing this survey, if your score was 0–4, you probably have no major stress problem at work that would influence your temperament. If your score was 6–14, you can be reasonably sure your work is having a negative impact on your stress level and temperament. If your score was 16 or higher, we urge you to seek professional help.

Many temporary or short-lived changes in your temperament can be simply the effects of mood, weather, or fatigue. However, more lasting changes in temperament or repeated changes in temperament may be due to stress.

The most damaging situation exists if you scored high in both personal and professional.

Figure 3.2 You can reduce your classroom stress level

You have looked at stress and temperament from viewpoints of personal and professional reactions. If you scored high in the personal questions section and low in the professional section, you probably have a personal problem or situation that needs correction. Likewise, if you scored high in the professional section and low in the personal section, your reactions to certain things at work are causing you great anxiety and affecting your temperament. The most damaging situation exists if you scored high in both the personal and professional areas. Don't feel alone if you have a stress problem or scored high in both areas. It is most difficult to be mechanical enough to turn off your problems from work when you get home or to avoid taking your personal problems to work. But relax, help can be found in the next section, "Reducing Stress Levels."

REDUCING STRESS LEVELS

You are now going to learn ways to reduce your stress level. Throughout this book, you will discover much about your priorities, how to deal with different personalities, and how to manage time more to your advantage. You will learn that by selecting the right things in determining your professional and personal priorities and by developing a plan to balance your time and to deal with conflict, your stress level can be reduced. Thus, good planning of the above can result in the *prevention* of much unneeded stress. However, when interruptions become too frequent, or when you become a casualty of the "time robbers" or poor planning, your attempts to prevent stress will be limited. At that point, you need to establish some stress reduction techniques. Before doing that, however, you need to determine the level of your stress.

First, look at the items listed below and check all symptoms you have experienced in the past two weeks. Next, place a SECOND checkmark by the symptom if it has occurred three or more times during the same period.

Box 3.2

SYMPTOMS

Headaches	Back pains	Irritation
Stomach pains	Dizziness	Sexual dysfunction
Indigestion	Extreme fatigue	✓✓Insomnia
Weight loss	Depression	✓Nervousness
Weight gain	Shortness of breath	Tightness in chest

Count each item checked as one point. Add one more point for each item with two checks.

Count EACH of the *first* checkmarks as one point, and add one point for EACH *second* checkmark. Add up your score.

According to pilot results, if you scored from 0 to 3, you probably do not have a stress problem. If you scored from 4 to 8, you may need to see a health professional and begin a stress management program. Scores between 9 and 15 could indicate that your stress capacity has been exceeded and you may be heading toward some serious problems and should see your personal health provider. *Please Note:* Any one of these symptoms could be unrelated to stress and be a serious problem in itself and may need to be checked by a health professional. Multiple symptoms definitely imply problems.

It is important to mention here that not all of the symptoms listed above are caused only by stress. Many minor and major illnesses can exhibit the same symptoms or combinations of symptoms. Likewise, other symptoms not listed, such as high blood pressure, numerous gastrointestinal problems, and unusual pains, can also be stress related.

If you have numerous symptoms or pain with any symptom, you should seek an appropriate health official as soon as possible.

Marty

Marty, a prosperous middle school teacher, was promoted to team leader. During the previous two years, Marty has gone through many stressful events. He has found that his principal is quite ineffective and lacks organization, and since Marty accepted the team leader position, the principal has delegated most problem areas to him. Marty is an excellent problem solver, but his boss has received most of the glory, including financial rewards, from Marty's work. Marty also has averaged more than sixty hours per week on the job and has never taken an appropriate lunch break. He has been unable to see any of his son's basketball games.

(Continued)

(Continued)

In addition to the sixty-plus hours at the office, Marty brings schoolwork home every day. His wife Ellen has become distant and goes out socially on her own. Marty has had periods of insomnia, a nagging headache that reappears almost daily, stomach problems compounded by daily periods of indigestion, and an unexplained weight loss of twelve pounds. Friends say he is nervous, appears fatigued all of the time, and is easily irritated. For the past month, Marty has become apathetic, missed work, and slumped into a depressed state.

Marty may have checked the symptoms as follows:

Box 3.3

MARTY'S SYMPTOMS

✓✓ Headaches	Back pains	✓✓ Irritation
✓✓ Stomach pains	Dizziness	Impotence
✓✓ Indigestion	✓✓ Extreme fatigue	Insomnia
✓ Weight loss	✓ Depression	✓✓ Nervousness
Weight gain	Shortness of breath	Tightness in chest

Total: Fourteen points. Marty has problems. He needs to reassess his priorities and perhaps seek professional medical assistance. Marty needs to determine if there is something else he could do, such as just teach or perhaps return to school to become a principal. He hopes he can rescue his marriage before it is too late. Although he may be able to make these improvements on his own, it will be most difficult. Marty will need much support. In fact, with the severity of his problem, he would benefit from appropriate professional guidance.

> You have three choices when thinking of ways to improve your life. ONE: You can accept things as they are and not make needed changes; TWO: You can quit work and become a monk or hermit; *or* THREE: You can modify your situation, make appropriate changes, and improve the quality of your life.

Such is the case with handling stress. Of course, *prevention* is the best situation. But when your prevention hasn't worked, strive to add activities to lower your stress level. You can describe any activities that lower your stress levels as *adaptive behaviors*— adaptive in that while you are involved in these activities your stress level is lowered and there are no negative or harmful results or side effects. Examples of adaptive behaviors are walking, listening to music, and biofeedback. Quite the opposite of adaptive behaviors are maladaptive behaviors. Maladaptive behaviors are activities you can use to lower stress levels but that have harmful or negative side effects, such as inappropriate use of alcohol, abuse of tranquilizers, smoking, and excessive eating. Obviously, adaptive behaviors are superior. In fact, such adaptive behaviors can have additional positive effects. For example, walking, swimming, and most exercises, in addition to lowering stress levels, can improve strength, flexibility, breathing, heart rate, and overall fitness.

For adaptive behaviors to be effective, you should select those that you find enjoyable. See the boxed List of Activities, which is by no means complete, through which you may *adapt your behavior* to lower your stress level.

As stated before, these examples are only a few suggestions to begin your thinking. Experiment and try several things until you find what is right for you. In addition to the above items, immediate *stress reducers* are available. However, we have learned what may be a stress reliever to one person, may be a stressor to another. For example, jogging is a perfect case.

Box 3.4

LIST OF ACTIVITIES

I. Exercise
- Walking
- Running
- Jogging
- Swimming
- Bicycling
- Tennis
- Dancing
- Martial arts

II. Sports/Recreation
- Softball
- Bowling
- Badminton
- Boating
- Skiing
- Camping
- Horseback riding
- Hiking

III. Music
- Listening to music
- Singing
- Playing a musical instrument

IV. Games
- Card games
- Computer games
- Board games

An activity that is stress reducing for one person may be stressful for another person.

PROFESSIONAL COPING STRATEGIES

While there are many individual strategies that teachers can use to help manage stress, there are also several professional methods that can aid in this battle. One of the most common professional factors teachers can manage with regard to stress reactions is perceived work demands. In the classroom perhaps the most effective ways to decrease experienced demands would be to reduce pupil misbehavior and coordination problems, reduce teachers' workloads, and stimulate teacher cooperation. For example, knowledge of the curriculum and knowing the structure, organization, and culture of the school can help students feel more comfortable in the classroom environment, thus reducing the amount of student misbehavior and correlated teacher stress.

One of the most common professional factors to be managed with regard to stress reactions among teachers is perceived work demands.

Research Note

Researchers offer some other professional coping strategies. For example, being well prepared for lessons and for the general responsibilities associated with life as a schoolteacher are important strategies in avoiding stress. The use of self-management skills such as preparation, planning, and organizational skills can also reduce stress in the classroom. Teachers who want to manage stress in the classroom may find that it is as simple as taking the time to talk with others.

Some of the best professional strategies are already in place before the teacher even sets foot in the classroom. These proactive strategies include avoiding employer/employee mismatches, realistic job previews, task-specific selection requirements, and good employee recruitment. During recruiting, human resource managers should avoid mismatches. A mismatch may result in heightened stress levels with deleterious effects on teachers, students, and school systems.

One way to reduce the gap between the personal expectations of newly recruited teachers and educational realities would be to use realistic previews as a recruitment tool. Similar steps should be applied in the selection process. An employer might carefully analyze the tasks involved in day-to-day classroom life in order to identify which skills are actually necessary to perform job tasks, and then use this analysis to restructure the selection procedure.

Good recruitment and task-specific selection can assist in reducing job stress as well. Effective use of accurate screening devices during the selection process helps ensure a better fit between individual abilities and the school system's job requirements. A mismatch between needs and abilities due to poorly conceived and executed recruitment and selection procedures can result in increased stress levels with negative effects on teachers, students, and school systems.

THE BENEFITS OF PHYSICAL EXERCISE

Stress does not have to lead to teacher burnout, if individuals can learn how to respond to and balance the accumulation of stress. There are numerous ways to deal with stress and return your body and mind to a state of balance or homeostasis. In this chapter we have focused on physical activities that are recognized by health professionals as stress reducers when used appropriately and regularly. We have included several physical activities that you can use to manage stress levels. These physical stress reducers, which can be practiced before, during, or after school, are effective activities that are usually selected based upon personal preference, perceived effectiveness, availability of materials and/or space, and proper training or guidance.

WARNING !

It is imperative that before beginning any exercise program you get approval from your doctor and have a complete physical.

As teachers we can use the time management skills we will learn in Step 4 to help us find time to exercise. Exercise helps to loosen the muscle tension created by stress. Exercise also takes our attention and concentration off stressful thoughts and helps us focus on the exercise and related skills. By increasing the exercise levels, we build up energy levels that strengthen us to be more effective in other aspects of our personal and professional lives.

Exercises ranging from a simple walk around the school to running miles to prepare for a marathon can help to lower blood pressure and heart rate, increase endurance, improve mood, decrease appetite, increase metabolism, and reduce excessive stress hormones, as previously discussed.

As our body becomes more resilient, stress is more easily managed simply because of the improved condition of our body. You will learn that sustained exercise and the related increase in endurance are critical components to managing stress. Endurance-creating exercise will help you to eliminate the physical symptoms that are identified with immediate and chronic stress.

Physical Activities During School Hours

Walking

Walking is a BEST exercise! While we walk several miles during a school day, this time is not focused on relieving stress. Finding ten minutes to walk around the gym during a duty-free lunch period or outside if that is feasible is an excellent way to calm down and get refocused. During this short ten or fifteen minutes, walk at your normal pace and breath slowly and deeply in and out through your nostrils as you walk.

Stretching

Nothing can be more immediately relaxing than five minutes of moderate stretching. While it is hard to find a space for floor positions, standing positions can be done in almost any space. One very easy position is to stand straight and with feet together, raise your arms and inhale as you lift . . . HOLD for a count of three . . . and then exhale and bring your arms down (see Figure 3.3). IMPORTANT: Stretch as far as you can *without* lifting your heels off the floor. Do this slowly and carefully. Repeat three or four times.

If you have a large towel or a mat, you can do a sit and stretch (see Figure 3.4). Be careful and go slowly. Sit with your feet close together in a comfortable position (remember, you are not doing a

Figure 3.3 Standing Stretch

major workout here, you are trying to relax). Next, inhale deeply and bend forward, S-L-O-W-L-Y exhaling as you lower your upper body. Reach outward with your hands and stretch and reach for your knees or shins. DO NOT PUSH HARD, AND DON'T GO AS FAR AS YOU CAN . . . just breathe and relax. Repeat three or four times.

Desktop Yoga

One of our favorites, desktop yoga, can be practiced literally at your desk or on your desk. You can do these activities with your

Figure 3.4 Sitting Stretch

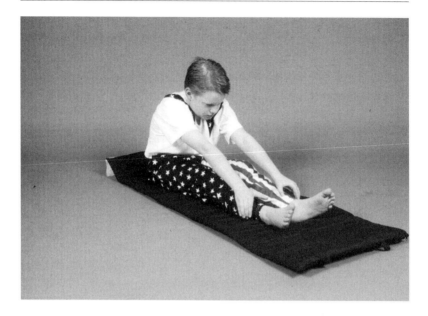

class. We teach this to people who have a hard time leaving a group. No special clothes are required and before you know it, everyone in the room or class will be doing these wonderful exercises (see Figure 3.5).

Correct Breathing

Before you begin, it is important that you breathe correctly for maximum benefits. Watch a baby breathe. A baby inhales as the diaphragm (even the stomach) rises or extends outward and lowers or comes inward as he or she exhales. That is normal breathing. We as adults have changed it. We tend to breathe the opposite way. Well, time to change.

In desktop yoga, you breathe in deeply as you inhale: RAISING or extending the diaphragm and stomach and LOWERING the diaphragm when exhaling. Let's experiment. Sit in a chair at your desk with your upper body straight and head up straight. Place your hand on your lower chest and inhale, drawing air into your lungs. You will feel your chest and stomach rise. Breathe in deeply and then exhale. Now you will feel your chest and stomach lower. Practice this

Figure 3.5 Desktop yoga can be practiced at your desk or on your desk.

several times. In fact, this is an excellent way to relax. Just sit and breathe for four or five minutes (see Figure 3.6). You will need to breathe in this manner when you do the desktop yoga exercises.

Sitting Tree

In Sitting Tree, sit at your desk (or on your desk with your legs crossed if that is comfortable) and begin the pose (see Figure 3.7).

Figure 3.6 For correct breathing, breathe in deeply as you inhale, raising or extending the diaphragm. Lower the diaphragm when you exhale.

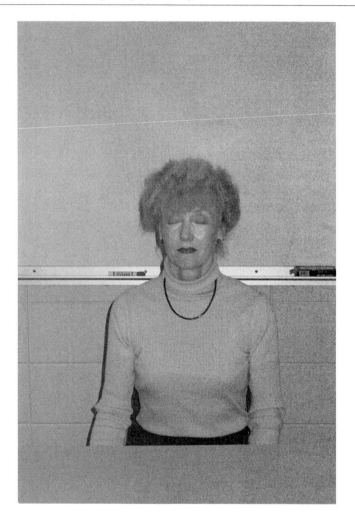

With your hands on your desk or by your sides, inhale deeply. As you exhale, slowly bring your hands upward until the palms of your hands touch. Practice this until you naturally get the last part of your exhaling to be at the point your palms touch. Your arms can be bent or straight. Sit in the tree position and inhale and exhale one full breath slowly and then inhale deeply and exhale as you slowly lower your arms. Repeat two or three times.

Figure 3.7 Sitting Tree

Turning Bird

This exercise is very relaxing and is great for students right
before an exam (see Figure 3.8). Sitting straight as you did when
practicing Correct Breathing, inhale deeply and then exhale as
you slowly lower your head gently forward. At the end of the
exhale, inhale deeply and exhale slowly as you bring your head to
a straight position. Next repeat by slowly dropping your head

Figure 3.8 Turning Bird is great for students right before an exam.

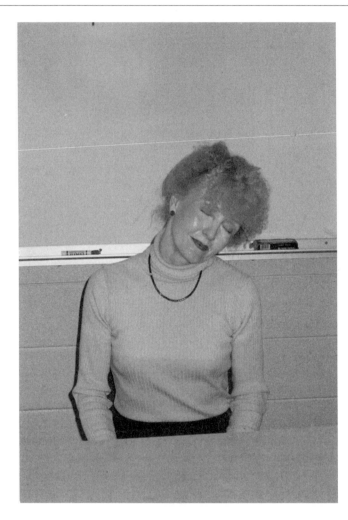

backward as you exhale, inhale, and return. Do the same with your neck to the left and then to the right.

If you get confused about breathing, just remember that you inhale deeply while you are still and exhale as you move. You have it! Just be careful and do not push hard or bend deeply.

The focus is on your breathing. You are relaxing, not warming up for a marathon. Some individuals like to close their eyes during this exercise. You may find that more relaxing as well.

Figure 3.9 Tired Warrior

Tired Warrior

Sit in your chair and inhale deeply with your arms at your sides (see Figure 3.9). As you exhale raise your arms upwards and slowly turn your head to the right. Hold and inhale deeply . . . exhale and lower your arms. Repeat, turning your head to the left. You can repeat this exercise two or three times on each side. Remember to exhale as you raise and lower your arms and turn your head.

Rising Cobra

For Rising Cobra, place your head on top of your hands (left hand on top of right hand) and take a few slow breaths (see Figure 3.10). Take a deep breath and as you begin to exhale raise your head, move your hands apart keeping them flat on the desk, and stop at the end of your breath with head extended backwards and your arms straight (see Figure 3.11). Inhale and exhale for one full breath. Now inhale deeply and exhale as you return slowly to the original position with your head on your hands. Sit and breathe two or three slow breaths, then repeat two or three times.

Figure 3.10 Rising Cobra: Begin with your head on top of your hands.

Nosey Neighbor

This exercise has two variations. The first is done sitting on your desk or on a towel or mat on the floor. Sit in a cross-legged position (or, if you are a yogi, in a half lotus or full lotus) with your hands on your knees and your head turned slightly to the right (see Figure 3.12). Inhale deeply and then exhale slowly as you turn your upper body (concentrate on your right shoulder and head) and head to the right. As you are exhaling and turning, bring your left hand to your right knee and place your right hand on the desk behind you for support (Figure 3.13). Inhale and then exhale as you return to the original position. Repeat to the left (Figure 3.14).

For the second method, sit in a chair. As you exhale and turn to the right, move your left hand to your right knee and grasp the edge of the seat with your right hand as you turn (Figure 3.15). Repeat to the left (Figure 3.16).

Alternate Breathing

This is an excellent sitting exercise. On the desk or in a chair, sit straight and place your right thumb and ring finger on each

Figure 3.11 Rising Cobra: As you exhale, raise your head and move your hands apart, stopping at the end of your breath with head extended backwards and arms straight.

side of your nose (see Figure 3.17). With your right thumb, gently close your right nostril and inhale deeply through your left nostril. As you start to exhale, close your left nostril with your ring finger, release your thumb, and exhale through your right nostril. Holding this position, inhale through your right nostril and as you

Figure 3.12 Begin Nosey Neighbor. Inhale deeply.

begin to exhale, close the right nostril with your thumb, release the ring finger, and exhale through your left nostril. Repeat several times.

If you get lost, remember that you inhale through one nostril, close it, and exhale through the other; then inhale through the same nostril you just exhaled through, close it, and exhale through the other side, then inhale, and so on. For additional information on desktop yoga visit us at www.frazzledteachers.com.

Figure 3.13 Exhale as you turn your upper body and head to
the right. Place your right hand on the desk
behind you for support.

Activities Before and After School

There are several physical activities you can do for stress relief
before and after school. Remember, before beginning any physical
exercises consult your health care professional. Once you get a
check-up or physical, there are two major points to remember

Figure 3.14 Return to your original position and then repeat the sequence to the left.

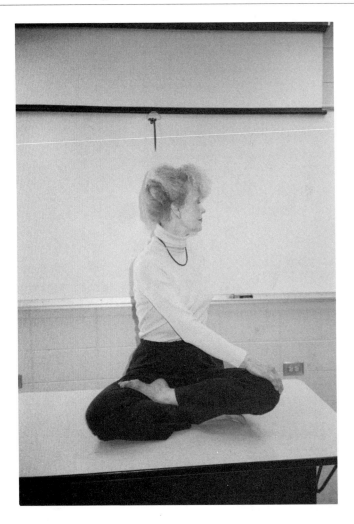

before beginning. The first is to have the proper dress, equipment, and instruction.

The second is to start and stay with a routine. Listed below are some excellent sports or activities to get involved with individually, with a partner, or as a member of a team or club.

- Walking
- Running

Figure 3.15 For Nosey Neighbor in a chair, move your left hand to your left knee and grasp the chair with your right arm as you turn.

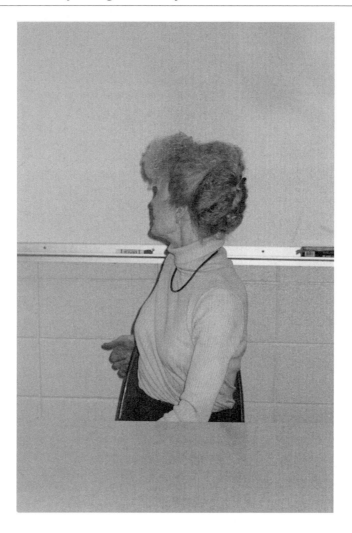

- Swimming
- Water aerobics
- Weights or resistance training
- Dancing
- Traveling

Figure 3.16 Return to your original position and then repeat the sequence to the left.

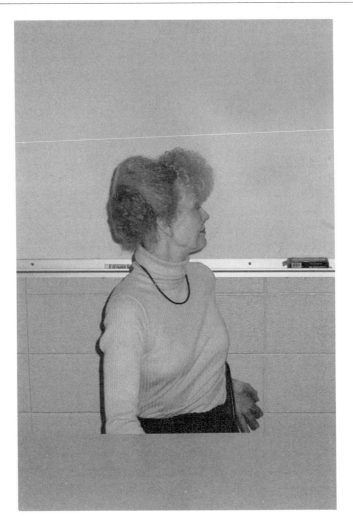

Physical Activities With a Different Twist

Yoga Classes

Our desktop yoga program is based on traditional yoga programs, which have become very popular in America. If you look in your community, you may find several different forms of yoga. Hatha yoga is the most popular and uses controlled breathing

Figure 3.17 For Alternate Breathing, inhale through one
nostril and exhale through the other.

techniques, postures, and movements for relaxation and improved
health. Yoga means "union" of the mind and body. Some forms
focus more on the mental aspects of yoga by focusing more on
meditation or spiritual aspects. People who practice yoga discover
improved health, reduced stress, and clearer thinking.

While many think of yoga as a New Age activity, the truth is
quite the opposite. Yoga has been around for hundreds of years.

Many consider that the great yogi Pantanjali, who lived around 200 B.C., was perhaps the first ever to write about yoga and the resulting benefits. Today, yoga instructors can be found in almost every city in the nation. Contact your local YMCA, community college, or community center to find a qualified instructor.

In addition, there are some excellent training tapes and CDs, yoga camps, retreats, and books that are regularly advertised in the *Yoga Journal,* which is published six times a year. We believe the videotapes and CDs with instruction by Patricia Walden and Rodney Yee are better for the beginning student. You can learn more about yoga and the popular journal, *Yoga Journal,* by visiting: www.yogajournal.com.

Pilates

Pilates is one of the latest physical exercises to hit the market. While not new, the pilates craze is being practiced as a way to relax the body and the mind. Pilates (pronounced, pi-LAH-teez) was developed by Joseph Pilates, a German boxer who brought the exercise to America in the 1920s. Movements used in Pilates focus on the muscles of the abdomen, lower back, and buttocks while using deep concentrated and correlated breathing. Five special pieces of equipment were developed by Pilates to help develop the muscles uniformly. The student or practitioner lies on a mat to do a series of stretches using the pulleys and other equipment to tense the muscles by using the person's own body and gravity to supply the needed resistance.

Joseph Pilates's exercise method incorporates more than 500 defined and controlled movements as well as elements of yoga and Zen meditation. Today the techniques used in Pilates are quite accessible from private instructors, fitness studios, and even hospitals. Physical therapists and sports teams are using Pilates for the benefits of strength, flexibility, and improved posture to help prevent sports injuries.

Most movements are done in sets of tens. Initially the Pilates method was designed for body alignment, injury prevention, and to build flexibility during rehabilitation. The movement has now expanded throughout the country and is promoted as a stand-alone sport. As with many types of sports that have developed in America, some of the focus has changed to accommodate the American lifestyle. Many centers teach Pilates as an advanced form of yoga, using only mats and not the equipment. Pilates intended his exercises to bring about a balance of mind and body. Individuals who practice Pilates report a reduction in stress levels in addition to an improved body.

> We caution individuals interested in Pilates to find a certified instructor who has completed the 600 hours of required training. We recommend that you begin with Pilates training only after locating a qualified instructor.

When done correctly, Pilates exercises can strengthen the trunk and pelvic area. They are a great tool for strengthening the lower back to avoid back strain problems related to stress. Enthusiasts report relief from all types of neck and back pain. Reports of Pilates being used to reduce pain from arthritis have been published.

> NOTE: Some find the Pilates exercises somewhat difficult at first, but with practice and qualified instruction, participants report improved posture and stronger muscle tone. One common finding was that Pilates users reported a reduction in stress levels after a few sessions.

> **For More Information:** To learn more about Pilates exercise, visit www.pilates.com.

Karate or Cardio Kickboxing

Karate is a martial art that was brought to the United States after World War II. Its origins are unclear, but many *karateka* (karate practitioners) believe that the ancestry of karate dates back a few thousand years to somewhere in India or China. Karate literally translated means "empty hands" and has evolved into a major sport throughout the world today.

Modern karate was developed by Ginchin Funakoshi, a schoolteacher from Okinawa, who later introduced it at several universities in Japan. Japanese karate evolved into several different styles, based upon some of the first great masters' interpretations of what would be best. Japan has four major styles today, including *Shotokan, Shito-ryu, Wado-ryu,* and *Goju-ryu* (*ryu* means school). From these styles, hundreds of other styles continue to be modified and developed.

Japan has not cornered the market on karate; China has several styles of Kung Fu, and Korea has Tae Kwon Do. American instructors have developed many variations and combinations to come up with American Karate. Perhaps the greatest martial artist of all time was a Kung Fu expert named Bruce Lee. Lee studied several forms of Chinese Kung Fu and boxing, and later developed a style that went against any of the orthodox styles or systems, Jeet Kwon Do (the Way of the Intercepting Fist), and taught this art form until his mysterious death in 1973 while filming a martial arts movie in Hong Kong.

Today you can study any type of karate that you desire, and unless you are interested in becoming a black belt, we can say the styles are basically similar. Karate students learn to use a series of arm blocks, kicks, punches, and strikes as a system of self-defense (see Figure 3.18).

In addition to self-defense, karate students use karate exercises for stretching and strengthening arm and leg muscles. Students with the same level of ability (belt color or rank) participate in sparring activities known as *kumite* (KOO-muh-TAY) for fun and in competitions held in almost any city in the world (Figure 3.19). The softer side of karate is a dance-like routine called forms or *kata* (KA-tuh). These are prearranged exercises from simple to complex. Funakoshi developed nineteen such *katas* that are still taught in the pure form by instructors certified by the Japanese Karate Association. Prizes and trophies are awarded to the best performers.

Closely related and perhaps somewhat dangerous is kickboxing. Kickboxing is usually full contact with a minimum of protective equipment. Another closely related sport is cardio kickboxing, which is usually just exercise in which only canvas bags are struck. While we don't recommend full-contact kickboxing, the cardio kickboxing workout can be awesome for relieving stress and getting into shape. You can even pretend the punching bag is an aggressive parent or your pri——— no, we are

Figure 3.18 Karate students learn to use a series of arm
blocks, kicks, punches, and strikes as a system
of self-defense.

not going there. We recommend Billy Banks's TaeBo workout, which you can practice in the privacy of your home. Visit www.taebo.com for more information.

If you decide to study karate for all of the benefits of sport, competition, belts, and so on, we strongly recommend that you find a qualified instructor and check out his or her credentials. If you take karate for fun, the same is true, but be sure that you are in a class that is focusing on karate for balance. Breathing, meditation, and the physical components can help to alleviate frustration, anger, anxiety, and shed unwanted pounds. Check out an instructor at the local gym or YMCA before paying $75 to $125 per month in fees. Have fun, but be careful. Wear loose-fitting clothes, such as a jogging or sweat suit, until you can order a karate suit (*gi,* pronounced *gee*). You can read more about karate in *Black Belt Magazine* and can find books for karate instructors for children by visiting www.writersedgepress.com.

Figure 3.19 Karate groups participate in sparring activities (*kumite*) and dance-like routines (*kata*) for fun and competition.

Other stress relieving activities with a different twist include Judo, T'ai Chi Ch'uan, Qi Gong, Shiatsu, and Reiki. Books on these topics can be found at your local bookstore.

Immediate Stress Management Techniques

In some situations you may find stress so intense that you lose control or feel as though you are going to lose control. Of course, as stated before, prevention is the best medicine. Even with prevention and leisure activities (e.g., exercise, music, etc.) you may not escape all negative stress. As you find yourself in a situation that suddenly increases your stress level or exceeds your stress capacity, such as during a lesson or after dealing with a difficult parent or a discipline problem, you can use what we call the Squeezer, the Breather, or the Calmer to gain immediate control. Each of these can also be done in more detail and for longer

---

Box 3.5

THE SQUEEZER

The Squeezer can be done as follows:

1. In a sitting or standing position, drop your arms heavily downward and let them just hang by your sides.

2. Squeeze your hands as though you have a lemon in each hand. Squeeze the imaginary lemons simultaneously, holding the *squeeze* firmly for a count of three. Repeat twice.

3. Now squeeze your hands and tighten your arms up to the shoulder level. Hold for a count of three.

4. Repeat two or three times.

---

periods of time before and after school. Of course, you will not go from a high, possibly explosive state to a completely calm state as in nirvana, but you will not explode, scream or shout, or walk away. You will regain your composure and maintain a high level of physical, mental, and emotional control.

You can become an expert in a few weeks and be able to squeeze and lock all muscles in your body for a count of three. As a form of deep muscle relaxation, the *Squeezer* allows the muscles to contract and relax, thus bringing you relief from stress. The more you practice this technique and the more of your body you include in this exercise, the greater the stress relief.

Warning: Individuals with high blood pressure, heart conditions, and other chronic conditions should seek their physician's advice before beginning this exercise due to the strenuous nature of the activity.

You may find the Squeezer is an important addition to your stress management program, especially in such situations as before and after stressful meetings, confrontations with employer or employees, and prior to a physical or mental contest. Most people prefer to do this activity in a private setting like their office, a rest room, or even a closet. Some people prefer the Breather because it is easier to do than the Squeezer. The Breather can be done as follows:

Box 3.6

THE BREATHER

1. Sit or stand quietly with your eyes closed. Hold your arms by your sides or in your lap.

2. Take a deep breath by inhaling through your nose. Hold for a count of three.

3. Push the breath out by exhaling through your mouth.

4. Repeat two or three times.

The Breather exercise in itself can be most relaxing. However, you may find that you would like to combine the Squeezer and the Breather for maximum benefits. To do so, complete the following:

Box 3.7

THE COMBO

1. Sit or stand quietly with your eyes closed and let your arms dangle by your sides with no resistance.

2. Inhale through your nose while completing the Squeezer technique. Hold and contract and lock muscles for a count of three.

3. Exhale through your mouth while relaxing your muscles.

4. Repeat two or three times.

You may also gain great benefit by using the Breather even in a crowded situation where you have no privacy, such as during a meeting or in a debate or argument. When this occurs, do the following:

Box 3.8

THE BREATHER 2

1. Inhale lightly through your mouth, inhaling continuously for maximum capacity, usually to a count of four or five.

2. Exhale lightly, but immediately, until the air is completely exhaled.

3. Repeat three or four times.

The success that can be found with the Breather is twofold. One, you are slowing down physically and mentally. Two, you are focusing physically and mentally on the breathing and not on the situation, person, or event causing the excessive stress.

The Calmer

Perhaps the most effective of all the immediate stress relievers is the Calmer, also called the Thinker. In the Calmer you let your mental processes direct and control your body in removing stress. This exercise takes about fifteen minutes to complete and is best done in a quiet, darkened room.

Box 3.9

THE CALMER

1. Sit or lie quietly with your eyes closed.

2. Memorize or record and play the Calmer (Thinker) dialogue.

3. Think of every direction in order as you remember, or think and concentrate as you listen to the recording of the Thinker dialogue. DO NOT SPEAK OR OPEN YOUR EYES DURING THE ACTIVITY.

THE CALMER DIALOGUE

(Deep breath, inhale . . . exhale)

I am sitting or lying quietly with my eyes closed. I am in control. I am in command of the stress I feel.
(Deep breath, inhale . . . exhale)

I feel a warm, comfortable feeling in my feet. My ankles, toes, and heels all feel warm, as though I am in a warm whirlpool. The stress is flowing out of my feet. My feet are relaxed. I am in control.
(Deep breath, inhale . . . exhale)

I now feel the relaxing, warm, comfortable feeling flow from my upper legs. The warmth is now at my hips. The warmth increases as it flows down my thighs, my calves, my ankles, and my feet. With the flow there is a most relaxing feeling, as though my body is in a warm hot tub or sauna. As this flow continues down my legs it pushes the stress from my hips, legs, and feet out of my body. I am relaxed from the waist down. I am in control.
(Deep breath, inhale . . . exhale)

Now I drop my arms limply by my side. From my neck I feel a warm, continuous, and relaxing feeling radiating down my back and chest. It continues down both my arms to the ends of my fingers, and down to my hips, legs, and out through my feet. I feel the flow of heat again, as though a warm shower is hitting me on the neck, down the chest and back, and down my entire body. I am completely relaxed from my neck to my toes. With each warm flow, stress is removed downward and out. I am in control.
(Deep breath, inhale . . . exhale)

Finally, I feel the warmth of the sun hit my head. The warmth is so relaxing. My breathing is slow. I am relaxing. As the warmth continues down my neck, back, hips, and legs I demand that any remaining stress be completely removed. I am now in a completely relaxed state. I will remain here for a few more minutes. I continue to breath slowly and calmly. I have controlled my stress. It no longer exists.
(Deep breath, inhale . . . exhale)

I am going to end this exercise, but I will continue to be relaxed. I know I can return to the Calmer whenever I become stressed again. At the count of three, I will sit up straight and slowly stretch. At the count of two, I will move around and become aware of my immediate environment. At the count of one, I will open my eyes and be completely alert, but extremely refreshed and relaxed. Now, three . . . two . . . one.

(Deep breath, inhale . . . exhale)

You should feel great. At first you may want to record the dialogue and play it back during the exercise. Or, you can order a personalized tape or CD in which we will use your name to direct you through the exercise or we will direct your class in the exercise. Go to www.frazzledteachers.com.

This is an excellent form of visual imagery that you can expand to thirty- to sixty-minute sessions in the quiet of your home, office, or classroom.

All three of these immediate stress relievers can be major components in the overall management of your stress level. Although these are primarily designed for times when stress is overwhelming, you can incorporate them into your daily schedule. You will find the Calmer useful in preventing your stress level from building during the day.

DEVELOPING A STRESS MANAGEMENT PLAN

A. LEVEL I. Prevention Techniques I Will Use
 1. *organization*
 2. *class rules / discipline / management*
 3. *communication w/ colleagues & admin*
 4. *voicing problems and concerns*
 5. *schedule programs on days I am at the other schools*

B. LEVEL II. Leisure/Recreation Activities I Will Use
 1. *daily walking*
 2. *weekly tennis*
 3. *reading daily for pleasure*
 4. *enjoying the scenery*
 5. *spending time w/ family*

C. LEVEL III. Immediate Stress Relievers I Will Use
    1. *The Calmer to get control of self*
    2. *The Breather*
    3. _____
    4. _____
    5. _____

D. List situations, people, schedules, and the like, that will
    assist me to be successful in Level I.
    1. *administration*
    2. *teachers*
    3. *schedule grade levels back to back*
    4. *schedule assemblies on Wed/Thurs AM*
    5. *post rules and discuss w/ students*

E. List situations, people, schedules, and the like, that will try
    to prevent me from being successful with Level I.
    1. *assemblies*
    2. *unplanned events*
    3. *admin/teacher undermining authority*
    4. *lack of planning time*
    5. _____

F. Plan of action to correct problems listed in Item E.
    1. *communicate concerns with admin.*
    2. *improve scheduling for following year*
    3. _____
    4. _____
    5. _____

G. List situations, people, schedules, and so on, that will assist
    me to be successful in Level II.
    1. *self motivation*
    2. *organization*
    3. *support groups*
    4. *husband/children*
    5. *my pets*

H. List situations, people, schedules, and so on, that will try to
    prevent me from being successful with Level II.
    1. *obligations at home*
    2. *daughter's sport schedule*

3. *my own motivation*

4. _____

5. _____

I. Plan of action to correct problems listed in Item H.
   1. *exercise at other times*
   2. *delegate more to family members*
   3. *have others monitor me*
   4. _____
   5. _____

J. List situations, people, schedules, and the like, that will assist me to be successful with Level III.
   1. *class breaks*
   2. *before and after school time*
   3. _____
   4. _____
   5. _____

K. List situations, people, schedules, and so on, that will try to prevent me from being successful with Level III.
   1. _____
   2. _____
   3. _____
   4. _____
   5. _____

L. Plan of action to correct problems listed in Item K.
   1. _____
   2. _____
   3. _____
   4. _____
   5. _____

By having a workable plan, knowing your strengths, being aware of pitfalls, and implementing procedures to alleviate problems, you will master stress.

Whether you develop your plan in a notebook, on a computer, or on note cards, find ways to implement and evaluate often and make any necessary adjustments.

Regardless of what you put in your plan and what methods you choose to reduce your stress levels, please consider adding a loving pet to your life. While it may take a few weeks to get used to having a pet, the research is clear that individuals who have dogs and cats to care for and love share a longer life than those who never had pets in their life. This is even more important for individuals who may be retired, who live alone, or who have lost a spouse. Whether the pet is pedigreed or a mixed breed from the pound, get a pet and find the love.

Arresting Time Bandits at Home and at School

Figure 4.1 Perfectionism, procrastination, and the inability to say "No" are the three major time bandits

THE THREE MAJOR TIME BANDITS

In our work in schools, universities, and in life generally, the three major time bandits or causes we have seen for time management problems are perfectionism, procrastination, and the inability to say "NO." If all three of these general time bandits are in full operation in your life, then time, stress, and priorities are all out of control. This can lead to a miserable existence, especially in the classroom.

The Need for Perfection

It is almost humorous to hear someone talk about getting it right. While the old cliché, "If its not worth doing right, then its not worth doing" has an element of truth, the extreme perfectionist may actually need to seek some professional help. Some groups, such as the baby boomer generation, have an engrained sense of doing things correctly. And with the modern-day pressures to do more, faster and better, the complications can multiply easily.

What Is Perfectionism?

Perfectionism, basically, is the desire to do something in a perfect manner. It goes beyond the ordinary time or energy exerted to complete a specific task. The true perfectionist is never completely satisfied with the end product, regardless of how many times it is revised.

While most of us have some perfectionist tendencies in varying degrees, perfectionism can become a general time robber or may produce several specific time robbers. For example, a third-grade teacher who continues to teach a math concept and repeats it over and over until the entire class understands it, has great difficulty moving on to the next concept with the total class. Most third-grade teachers would move on with the class and work independently with the few who are having difficulty. What can be interesting is that the same third-grade teacher may have no problem moving forward in reading with the identical students who may have difficulty with a specific reading skill.

At home, signs of perfectionism may be that the house always has to be in order, the car always clean, or every last dish washed.

Perfectionism takes many forms as time bandits robbing you of extra time, leading you away from your priorities, and creating greater emotional stress.

> The perfectionist's greatest enemy is an unrealistic personal or professional agenda.

Dealing With Perfectionism

Perfectionists have problems meeting their own expectations, and even more meeting the expectations of superiors. However, it has been our experience that when external pressures are increased—such as an ultimatum to increase test scores or reach the expectations of requirements included within *No Child Left Behind*—they may actually encourage a perfectionist to create expectations that in fact exceed the requirements. Failure not to exceed the requirements causes the perfectionist to feel great pain. The time limits often run out for the perfectionist and the external expectation is not met, which can lead to the teacher feeling like a failure. Usually when this occurs, the individual affirms that, "Next time I will do it right," which reinforces the pattern of perfectionism. Some perfectionists feel they have to be the best at all times—which is another, related problem.

The best way to deal with perfectionism is to do more reality checks. For example, when facing a task like writing up a report for an accreditation agency such as SACS or a system report for the school, check with other individuals to see what their PERCEPTION of the task is and compare it with your own. Assuming these individuals are good teachers who are professionals and do what needs to be done, check the differences in perception. If you find that you are expecting much more than they are, it could be that you have a tendency toward perfectionism. Try realigning your perception with theirs and complete the task. You may find this difficult at first, but if you realign every time the urge "not to let go" hits, in no time you will have adjusted the way you complete tasks. If after several attempts at doing this you feel depressed or unimportant or a failure, we urge you to consult your health care professional.

Procrastination

What is procrastination? Procrastination is a specific time bandit that encourages you to "put off" a task, meeting, assignment, or lesson until a later time. Procrastinators usually take on too many tasks, and many are perfectionists as well. Sometimes the procrastinator just does not want to do the task, which is often an inability to say "No" to start with.

However, most teachers who are procrastinators feel overwhelmed and often work around the task, secretly hoping it will just go away. The tasks that are most often put off to the last minute are the big items. For example, your principal now wants your lesson plans two weeks in advance and you are so busy just getting through this week. The plans are due Friday afternoon and it is now Monday morning. You rationalize in your mind that you will have time during Friday morning planning to do the entire plan. So, you forget about it until then.

Several things may happen. You are called to cover a sick teacher's class during your planning period. You have an angry parent at your door demanding to talk with you. You sit down and start writing the plans and realize the planning time is over and you are only half finished, or you do the plans quickly, without detail, and the principal sees you on Monday and demands that these be done correctly. These are just a few of the scenarios that may occur.

In other situations, individuals may seriously plan to do a major task, but decide to get other smaller things completed before getting to the bigger item. In most cases, the small tasks get completed but the larger task is delayed further.

> The procrastinator's greatest enemy is unexpected events.

Why Do I Procrastinate?

Basically, for the same reasons listed above. One way to check how much you procrastinate is to keep a journal for two months and write down your thoughts about things you are delaying. Be honest with yourself. Write down your feelings of why you think you are procrastinating. Do you disagree with the task or assignment? Is it something you dislike? Are you letting the time bandit of being a perfectionist join forces with the time bandit of being a procrastinator? Are you hoping to avoid the task? Do you want to do the task but feel overwhelmed? If so, how does this make you feel? Are you capable of saying NO when you are already overloaded? After two months, perhaps before, if you stay loyal to recording your thoughts in your journal, you will see one of the above problem areas or a specific pattern. Once you know why you procrastinate, you can begin to deal with the problem.

One pattern we see for classroom teachers who procrastinate is being overwhelmed. They either can't say no to extra curricular responsibilities—OR they think they can't say no.

Another technique for dealing with procrastination is to break large tasks into smaller components. Try to complete the small parts in a timely manner, and before you know it you will have the big task completed.

Inability to Say "No"

The third and perhaps the most difficult time robber to battle is the inability to say "NO" or to say it and really mean it. In our social life we may feel that if we say no to someone asking us to do something specific in the community, church, or club, that we will not be liked or be perceived as not caring. If you are the type that worries about what other people think—what we call the WOPT Complex—your priorities will continue to suffer and so will your time. You are already stressed.

Usually there are three types of reactions that emerge from "I Can't Say No" in a social setting. The first is that you really don't want to do what is being asked of you, but you don't want to hurt someone's feelings or be thought of as not caring. After you agree to do the task, you find yourself angry at being stuck with the project that you did not want to do and did not have time to do. So, you complete it and give up priority time, which increases your stress. The second reaction to emerge is not saying no and then finding yourself procrastinating finishing the task until you are losing sleep or time with your family and wind up completing the task at the last minute under increased stress. The third reaction is accepting the task and then trying to find someone else during the eleventh hour to assist you to get it done. In this scenario, you

Figure 4.2   Personal and professional time management
strategies can help you outrun your time bandits.

are using people's good will to get you out of a mess. The smart
ones will say no to you next time if they see your intent.

Rules to Follow in Saying No

1. Respond politely with a smile but state that you will be
   unable to accept the task.
2. If pressured, repeat more firmly with a "NO" that you are
   unwilling to do the task.
3. If still pressured, remind the person that you have already
   said no and that you will not be changing your mind. Then
   politely excuse yourself.

PERSONAL AND PROFESSIONAL TIME MANAGEMENT STRATEGIES

The first thing we recommend is to keep all of your activities
(professional and personal) in one calendar either by electronic
means like a palm-top or other computer, or a more traditional

pen-and-paper calendar. We know educators who still prefer a notebook. The means is not important. What is important is using it appropriately.

One great technique to manage time better at home is to mark personal time and/or family time in your calendar first. The *Advanced Planning Method* (APM) is just like planning your vacation. Most of us mark our vacations and holidays off first thing when we get a new calendar. The APM approach is similar in that you go through your calendar on a weekly, or at least monthly, basis and mark periods of time that are for your personal and/or family time. You probably listed more personal time or more time with your family as major priorities. If so, you have to make time for the priorities. Mark out at least one hour per day just for you. Try to mark out between thirty and forty-five minutes per day for family. As you learn to avoid procrastination, perfectionism, and the inability to say no you will have more time. You will also become quicker at labeling the things that are more important.

Another method is the ABC Method. To use this approach, think from a weekly perspective and pick a day, usually Friday or Sunday, and plan the week ahead. Make three columns on a page. Label the A column *High Priority and Urgent*. Label column B *High Priority and Important*, and C as *Important but Not Urgent.*

Make one list of all the tasks that you have to do during the next week and then categorize each item into one of the three columns. Be sure to check your priority lists and include these items in the appropriate columns. For example, if you said you were going to walk thirty minutes each day, list that as a High Priority and Urgent task. If it falls under C, it stands less chance of happening.

Develop your own system using the ABC Method such as adding days across the columns or adding specific times of the day for the tasks. Some will already be scheduled, like faculty meetings or staff development. The real goal here is to lower the number of High Priority and Urgent tasks by completing as many of the High Priority and Important tasks as possible before they become High Priority and Urgent. This cuts down on time problems and prevents stress.

Other time management strategies include analyzing tasks that have to be done at home and delegating these tasks fairly. Many teachers end up teaching all day and then coming home to clean house, prepare dinner, and wash dishes and clothes. Divide these tasks and be firm in sticking to the plan. Remember, everything that you eliminate from your list of duties means more time for you.

Here are some more tips for reducing stress by managing time better:

Reducing Driving Stress

- Give yourself more time to get where you are going (add an extra five minutes for every twenty minutes of expected time, ten minutes in heavy city traffic).
- Stay focused on driving and listen to soft music.
- Be patient and keep a good sense of humor.
- Don't use your cell phone.

Working With Difficult Colleagues

- Inform them directly without being confrontational that what they are doing is bothering you or taking your time or causing you stress. Be assertive, but not aggressive.
- If the behavior does not improve, ask for a conference with the principal.
- Remember that some people will never change. You may be the one who has to change or leave the area to get the peace you need.

Improving Communication Problems

- Really listen and try to understand the person's viewpoint.
- Avoid "you" statements that can seem to attack.
- Watch your own body language.
- Be assertive without being aggressive.
- Learn to say NO and mean it.

SOME ADDITIONAL CLASSROOM TIME SAVERS

- Plan at least three weeks in advance.
- Leave later on Friday to get things ready for next week (good investment of time).

- Use the ABC Method above and include instructional activities and meeting times.
- Propose in a faculty meeting that walk-throughs be planned for certain days and times.
- Ask for a moratorium on use of the intercom during instructional time.
- Ask for a week's notice for class pull-outs.
- Have a parent volunteer to collect fees or book-order and picture money.
- Seek to get a rule that parents must schedule an appointment in advance.
- Ask for assistance in record keeping.
- Expect and demand that students return from pull-outs as scheduled.
- Use class helpers for filing and doing clerical tasks.
- Stay with your routine; expect other teachers to do the same.
- Seek creative ways to deal with noninstructional duties.
- Ask that faculty meetings be limited to one per month.
- Ask for a schoolwide discipline plan.
- Before agreeing to incentive programs, make sure additional help will be provided.
- Use student-led conferences instead of individual teacher conferences.
- Develop a buddy system with one or two teachers to cover class or other situations during a personal emergency or unexpected time robbers.

Keep adding to the list and share more with us and other teachers on the exchange board that can be found on our websites: www.frazzeledleaders.com.

STEP FIVE

Using Nutrition to Support a Healthy Lifestyle

Figure 5.1 The foods we choose to eat affect our health in a multitude of ways.

> **Food sustains life.**

NUTRITION AFFECTS TEACHERS' HEALTH

We need food in order to survive. Food gives us the important nutrients, vitamins, minerals, carbohydrates, fats, proteins and water that are needed for the everyday processes that the body is expected to perform. However, the foods that we choose to eat on a daily basis affect our health in a multitude of ways. Nutritious food in the proper amounts, such as that exhibited on the USDA's (United States Department of Agriculture) food guide pyramid, can greatly enhance the energy that we have to complete life's demanding tasks and have serious potential for warding off the deadly diseases that plague so many Americans. Teachers, in particular, are one group of professionals that have documented health-related problems as well as low job performance due to a lack of energy, more popularly phrased.

Research Note

Individuals under stress need to examine the consumption of food at each meal. Consumed food has a direct impact, either positively or negatively on a person's health. A healthier person has a much higher tolerance for stress than an unhealthy person does. Modifying a diet reduces salt, sugar, and caffeine intakes; includes eating a healthy breakfast; cuts back on the consumption of whole milk products; increases fiber intake; keeps alcohol intake at one or fewer beverage servings for a female and two or fewer servings for a male (if alcohol is a normal part of a daily diet); and changes how the body copes with stress. A healthy diet allows the body to deal with stress in a more positive way. Turkington reports that individuals with a stressful lifestyle should eat calcium-rich foods such as dairy products, and vitamin-rich foods such as fruits and vegetables. Many nutritionists believe that, for weight management, appropriate amounts of complex carbohydrates found in potatoes, rice, and dried beans are better than simple

(Continued)

(Continued)

carbohydrates found in most fruits and fruit juices. Individuals should also eat whole-grain bread and other grains containing vitamin B. Also, it is important that people experiencing stress eat at least three balanced meals a day. Things that counteract healthy eating and trigger stress are bingeing, seesaw dieting, irregular eating patterns, and consistent overeating. Ultimately, consuming the proper amounts of food and water is a top priority when recovering from stress. If the individual's nutritional needs are not met, stress becomes more pronounced, and all attempts to eliminate stress fail (Loehr, 1997). With a healthy daily diet, the body is able to resist stress instead of being attacked by stress.

There is no denying that teachers are under an incredible amount of stress. Teachers cannot afford to allow stress to compound without release; this is simply unhealthy. Fortunately, there are numerous physical activities that can be implemented on a short-term or long-term basis to reduce stress. Choosing a physical activity that best suits the individual is the key to surviving teacher stress. Refer back to Step 3.

What is nutrition and, more important, what is good nutrition? Nutrition is the manner in which the body makes use of food. This includes not only eating the correct amounts and kinds of foods, but also the processes by which the body uses food substances for growth, repair, and maintenance of body activities. Good nutrition refers to eating the proper amounts of nutrients that the body needs on a daily basis for energy and for all body processes. The body gets vital nutrients from foods. Vitamins, minerals, carbohydrates, fats, protein, and water are essential nutrients that the body needs for life. The mostly widely accepted guide is the USDA's Food Guide Pyramid, which gives recommendations for the kinds and amount of foods to be eaten daily to ensure that the proper amounts of nutrients are received by the body for optimal health.

The USDA's Food Guide Pyramid consists of five food groups and is intentionally shaped like a pyramid. The foods on the bottom are in the grain group and need to be consumed in larger amounts. This group provides the body with essential nutrients such as vitamins, minerals, and complex carbohydrates, and as such this group should form the foundation of a healthy diet. In contrast, the foods at the top of the pyramid—fats, oils, and sweets—should be consumed sparingly. These foods do not form a food group, and while fat is an essential nutrient, it is needed by the body in only small amounts.

Please note there is much disagreement and discussion on carbohydrates versus fats for health and proper nutrition. Most of the discussion centers around the Atkins Diet, which is focused on limiting carbohydrates and increasing protein and fat.

> *Nutrition* refers to the foods that contain the essential nutrients that are needed by the body for all of life's processes. Good nutrition refers to the foods that people eat that provide the body with the proper amounts of these nutrients to maintain a healthy life.

How Does Good Nutrition Affect Our Health?

We need to eat in order to survive, and the foods we choose impact our bodies' abilities to fight off diseases and other potentially deadly health problems. Choosing the foods near the base of the Food Guide Pyramid, like grains and fruits and vegetables, and limiting the foods at the tip of the pyramid can help people to look and feel their best while warding off some of the deadliest diseases of Americans, such as heart disease, cancer, diabetes, and stroke. Blood pressure, cholesterol level, tooth decay, anemia, skin, hair, and energy levels are all affected by our eating habits. Some nutritionists suggest instead of three regular meals daily, choosing a variety of foods that are low in fat, low in sugar, low in salt, and that contain essential nutrients, as well as eating in moderation and having several small meals a day are the keys to proper nutrition. No substantiated research is available that states whether either of these approaches is best. The basic keys are good selection of foods, a healthy balance of fats, proteins, and carbohydrates, and a normal calorie range (usually 2,000 calories daily). In addition, moods and feelings can influence our choices about what we eat. It is very easy for people to use food as a way to reduce stress, relieve boredom, combat fatigue, and as a means for socialization.

Eating in response to stimuli other than the feeling of hunger can lead to bad eating habits and poor nutritional choices. A lack of good nutrition can impact a person's ability to lead a healthy, happy, and productive life and can limit that person's ability to meet his or her personal and professional potential.

Teachers and Eating Habits

Lifestyle risk behaviors such as smoking, stress, drug abuse, poor nutrition, and physical inactivity contribute to almost one half of all deaths in the United States. The health status of school employees mirrors that of the American public. According to the American Association of School Administrators, one out of every six teachers has high blood pressure, one of every two is obese, and one of every ten has a substance abuse problem.

> Mr. Williams, a teacher in Austin, Texas, reflects the feelings of many teachers:
>
> "Doctor, I feel burned out at my job," I said to my physician, explaining that I felt great in the morning, but tired and grumpy by the afternoon. . . . Already that day I had taught for eight hours, photocopied 200 sets of papers for my team, laminated letters for my bulletin board, attended a faculty meeting, and prepared manipulatives for the next day's math lesson. I had scarfed down lunch, and was planning to heat up a frozen dinner.

This teacher had tried to battle fatigue with a mid-afternoon sweet treat, as do many teachers who reach for that candy bar or cupcake as a quick fix. The birthday and holiday parties, the daily sweets offered in the teachers' lounge and the cafeteria, the staff breakfasts consisting of doughnuts and coffee on staff development days, the candy fund-raisers, and the ice cream offered as a special "snack" or as an end-of-the-day "social" to provide additional funds to the school all take their toll on teachers' nutritional health. When teachers are faced with lunch times before 10:30 and little time in which to eat, the low-nutrition foods that are offered on a daily basis become hard to resist. Like Williams, many teachers have little or no time for a healthy, well-balanced lunch and are too tired by the end of the day for a nutritious dinner. Unlike other professions, teachers do not get a quiet, relaxing, hour-long (or even half-hour long) lunch break. Lunch consists of a twenty-minute period of time in which to "scarf" down something quick while simultaneously opening milk cartons, monitoring students' behaviors, breaking up arguments, listening to incessant chatter and high volumes of social interactions, trying to ensure that students are getting their proper nutrition at lunch, and cleaning up after students before the next class arrives. Hurried and emotional times like this have a major influence on the food choices people make. Another teacher explained that there are times when our emotions seem to demand more food than we need. Often the food we choose is the wrong kind. Unfortunately, we gravitate to sweets, breads, and fatty foods as false rewards for hard work. Satisfaction is temporary and within hours many are eating again.

In previous generations—and still today—a child was given candy and sweet treats as a special reward or privilege for a job well done. After a hard day's work in the education profession it is difficult to transcend that mentality, as evidenced by many personal admissions. It is no wonder with the constant pressure, stress, availability of sweet, sugary, low-nutrition foods, and their lack of time for slowing down, that teachers have so many health-related problems.

MAKING GOOD CHOICES

There are ways for teachers to overcome these unhealthy urges. Teachers can deal with a lack of energy and can combat fatigue and burnout by researching good nutrition and foods that can increase energy levels and by changing their current eating habits. We know that high-sugar foods cause a surge in energy followed by a drop. Coming down from a sugar rush can cause irritability and fatigue.

Deficiencies in essential vitamins and minerals could lead to feelings of fatigue. Eating iron-rich foods and foods rich in the vitamin B complex and folic acid help to reverse these effects. It is important though not surprising to note that many of the foods found to combat fatigue—like radishes, raisins, whole-grain breads, apples, pasta, most vegetables, and lean proteins—are not always readily available and it is easier to select high-fat meals from fast food restaurants.

Choosing Healthy Snacks

There are other things that educators can do to help assure proper nutrition. Eating raw fruits and vegetables is not only quick and easy, but also provides essential nutrients to the body and increases energy levels. Bringing a sandwich lunch of lean meat and low-fat cheese, along with fruits and vegetables can also be a healthy substitute for the many sugary, sweet treats offered in the cafeteria.

When teachers come into the lounge feeling hungry, tired, and stressed, it's so tempting to grab a sweet roll or a few cookies. Preplanning, however, can assist teachers in making wiser selections on a regular basis. Teachers who bring their favorite healthy snacks to school are able to avoid everyday lounge temptations, satisfy the need for a snack, and keep their eating habits on track.

Avoiding Temptation

Teachers, in particular, face many challenges and hurdles in the struggle for good nutrition. Good nutrition plays a key role in everyone's health and, above all, it is a choice that we make. It is important to realize that this choice not only affects one's own personal body but also impacts the students. Classroom instruction is affected by the daily nutritional choices that teachers make. Nutrition, exercise, and stress relief play major roles in the overall wellness of educators and in feeling good about oneself. Feeling good about oneself is associated with being a better parent, spouse, friend, and teacher. Lower absentee rates and increased productivity, time, and continuity on students' tasks are all improved when teachers feel good about themselves and are nutritionally healthy (Cox and Billingsley, 1996). Further, teachers who are self-motivated and energetic are more effective and able to get more accomplished than teachers who are tired and struggling just to think.

Nel Noddings writes that "teaching requires tremendous amounts of physical and psychic energy. When we as teachers can maintain a high level of energy, we can be powerful educators. We may even have the strength and ability to change schools for the better (personal communication, 2003)."

Good nutrition impacts more than the way people feel about themselves. Balancing the right kinds and amounts of foods can increase energy levels and help prevent teacher burnout.

Teachers who maintain high levels of energy are able to devote more to their profession to help ensure the success of all their students, while teachers who are sluggish and tired have little energy to give to themselves and less left over to give to their students.

Although good nutrition plays a decisive role in the health of teachers and in the effectiveness of their classroom instruction, there are other factors related to nutrition that also work to limit or enhance these qualities for educators.

Nutrition, Stress, and Exercise

Two major factors we will briefly discuss are exercise and stress. Stress has a major impact on the health of teachers and on the effectiveness of their instruction. Stress can leave a previously successful teacher feeling tired, unmotivated, inadequate, and ineffective. Lozada (2000) recently stated, "There are at least 50 common symptoms of stress . . . , including back pain, digestive problems, insomnia, fatigue, unexplained weight gain or loss and skin irritations." In addition there is a "very clear relationship between stress and the incidence of heart attacks and hypertension." Further, "more than 66 percent of all visits to primary care physicians are for stress-related disorders."

Though stress can limit the effectiveness of teachers' classroom instruction, exercise and good nutrition can combat these ill effects. The Clemson University Cooperative Extension Service states, "Your ability to cope with stress is affected by [your] nutritional status. Poor nutrition before and during high periods of stress will make you more likely to develop health problems and will reduce your ability to cope with stress" (*Nutrition and Stress*, n.d.).

You should pay attention to getting all the nutrients your body needs by eating a variety of foods, including fruits, vegetables, whole-grain and enriched breads, cereals and other grain products, milk, cheese, yogurt, meat, poultry, fish, eggs, and dry beans and peas.

Further, in addition to good nutrition, exercise is a beneficial way to help alleviate the stress that accompanies teaching. Many teachers who have regular exercise programs report feeling less tired and having more energy to devote to their students and to their professional careers. In addition, the combination of exercise and good nutrition has a more positive impact on health-related diseases than does nutrition alone. When good nutrition is supplemented with regular physical activity, the impact that stress has on the body and mind can be significantly reduced. As the American Dietetic Association points out, "The combination of nutrition and physical activity are also a primary strategy for reducing risk of coronary heart disease, hypertension, diabetes, and osteoporosis" ("For a Healthful Lifestyle," 1999). Exercise is beneficial to teachers because it helps alleviate the tiredness and frustration that lead many teachers to becoming emotionally drained and burned out by the many demands of the job. Teachers who participate in regular physical exercise have increased energy, a more positive outlook on life, and an ability to cope more effectively with stress. Physical fitness also acts as a preventive against serious health problems such as heart disease, high blood pressure, and obesity. Higher morale, increased productivity, and reduced rates of absenteeism are important to the teaching profession. Because of its many benefits, exercise is an important factor that you should explore when considering the role of nutrition on teachers' health and classroom instruction.

Good nutrition plays a key role in the health and quality of classroom instruction of teachers. When good nutrition is combined with daily exercise, the resulting effects are even more positive on teachers' health and effectiveness of classroom instruction.

> Both good nutrition and exercise help to combat stress, fatigue, burnout, and dangerous health-related disorders and diseases.

Unfortunately this is not an area of focus for many of us in schools. We are so busy! Even though the need clearly exists, few schools have implemented health promotion programs or have taken the initiative to offer health education and proper nutritional information in an effort to help teachers. In addition, few school principals realize the significance of good nutrition and how it impacts teachers' personal health and classroom instruction. Poor nutrition has been linked with increased absenteeism and increased doctor visits, which do impact the efficiency of the school system. Further, poor nutrition impacts classroom instruction in that teachers are less energetic, less motivated, and less able to get the job done to the best of their abilities. In the big picture, a few dollars spent on educating teachers about the benefits of good nutrition and daily exercise would have a positive impact on not only teachers' health and students' level of instruction, but also on school leaders' need to have motivated, energetic, positive, and effective teachers who come to school ready to do their job the best they can.

Teaching and Health

Teaching and health are interrelated. Teachers tend to mirror the health risks of the American public. If we as teachers can improve our state of health and quality of life, our students will benefit, and as a nation we will all benefit.

Body mass index (BMI) is frequently used by health professionals to determine whether an individual is underweight, of normal weight, overweight, or obese. These categories correlate with an individual's health risk status. For example, an individual whose BMI is in the category of Class I obesity would have a higher health risk status than an individual who was in the overweight category. One's BMI can be calculated by using the following mathematical formulas:

$$BMI = \frac{\text{weight in kilograms}}{\text{height in meters}^2} =$$

If you don't want to convert pounds to kilograms (2.2 lbs = 1 kg) and inches to meters (39.37 inches = 1 meter), you can use the alternate formula:

$$BMI = \frac{\text{weight in pounds}}{\text{height in inches}^2} \times 703 =$$

Not a math teacher? Use this Web site for calculation of your BMI:

www.caloriecontrol.org/bmi.html

A BMI between 18.5 and 24.9 is considered normal. Overweight individuals have a BMI between 25 and 29.0, and obesity is defined by a BMI greater than 30.

Blood lipid measurements include *cholesterol* and *triglycerides* and are used to screen for risk factors for coronary artery disease. Cholesterol screening is usually broken down into HDL (high density lipoproteins) and LDL (low density lipoproteins). Generally, total cholesterol levels below 200 mg/dl, LDL levels less than 130 mg/dl, and triglycerides between 40 and 150 mg/dl are considered within normal ranges. Normal HDL levels vary with sex, with normal male values being between 35 and 65 mg/dl and female between 35 and 85 mg/dl. Lifestyle factors that increase total cholesterol are a high-fat diet, lack of regular exercise, and stress. Excessive alcohol use and obesity can contribute to an increase in triglycerides. Since an HDL level above 35 is desired, individuals need to avoid lifestyle factors that will lower the HDL level: smoking, obesity, and physical inactivity.

Blood glucose levels are measured in a fasting state, when the individual has not had anything to eat or drink except water or black coffee. A normal blood glucose result is between 60 and 110 mg/dl. This test measures how the body metabolizes carbohydrates. If the individual has a higher-than-normal fasting blood glucose, further tests are required to determine if diabetes is present.

More than fifty million Americans have *elevated blood pressure* or hypertension. Blood pressure is the force exerted to move blood as the heart pumps blood through the vessels of the body. It is expressed as a ratio of systolic pressure over diastolic pressure—for example, 120/70. Hypertension is not diagnosed by one blood pressure reading alone, since anxiety in a clinical setting may cause the blood pressure to rise. For this reason, individuals are encouraged to have their blood pressure assessed frequently to detect whether there is a rising pattern in their blood pressure. Hypertension is defined as the systolic (first number) more than 140 mmHg or the diastolic (second number) over 90 mmHg. Since hypertension is linked to coronary artery disease, stroke, kidney failure, congestive heart failure, and other serious disorders, early diagnosis and treatment are essential.

Balanced nutrition, stress management, time management, and a healthy lifestyle can help all teachers lead long, creative, productive, and less frazzled lives.

Bibliography

Abel, M. H., & Sewell, J. (1999). Stress and burnout in rural and urban secondary school teachers. *The Journal of Educational Research, 92,* 287–296.

Alder, J. (1997). *Stress: Just chill out!* Springfield, NJ: Enslow Publishers.

Anderson, C. (1999). Time well spent. *Teaching PreK-8, 29,* 80(2).

Ayer, E. (1998). *Everything you need to know about stress.* New York: Rosen Publishing.

Barratt, H. (2002, June). Exams could worsen asthma. *Student BMJ, 10,* 175.

Borreen, J., & Niday, D. (2000, October). Breaking through the isolation: Mentoring beginning teachers. *Journal of Adolescent & Adult Literacy, 44*(2), 152.

Brodkin, A. M., & Coleman, M. F. (1994). Equip kids to deal with disaster. (Dealing with post-crisis stress in school children). *Instructor, 103,* 17–19.

Buell, J. (2001, Spring). The politics of time. *Independent School, 60*(3), 74–80.

Cohen, S. (1997). De-stress for success. *Training and Development, 51*(11), 76–80.

Cox, C., & Billingsley, J. (1996). Rationale for schoolsite health promotion. *Education, 116,* 514(5).

de Anda, D., & Bradley, M. (1997). A study of stress, stressors, and coping strategies. *Social Work in Education, 19,* 87–99.

Dounay, J. (2000, May). High-stakes testing is high-stress, too. *Education Digest, 65*(9), 9–14.

Dunham, J., & Varma, V. (Eds.). (1998). *Stress in teachers: Past, present and future.* London: Whurr.

Engelbrecht, P., Swart, E., & Eloff, I. (2001, November). Stress and coping skills of teachers with a learner with Down's syndrome in inclusive classrooms. *South African Journal of Education, 21*(4), 256–260.

Fanning first-year fires: Veteran educators provide year-long mentoring to guard against new-teacher burnout. (1998, October). *NEA Today, 17*(2), 23.

For a healthful lifestyle: Promoting cooperation among nutrition professionals and physical activity professionals. (1999). *Journal of the American Dietetic Association, 99*(8), 994.

Gaziel, H. H. (1993). Coping with occupational stress among teachers: A cross-cultural study. *Comparative Education, 29,* 67–80.

Glickman, C. D., Gordon, S. P., & Ross-Gordon, J. M. (2001). *Supervision and instructional leadership: A developmental approach* (5th ed.). Needham Heights, MA: Allyn & Bacon.

Gold, J., Thornton, L., & Metules, T. J. (2001, December). *Simple strategies for managing stress. RN, 64*(12), 65–67.

Goliszek, A. (1987). *Breaking the stress factor.* Winston Salem, NC: Carolina Press.

Graves, D. (2001). *The energy to teach.* Portsmouth, NH: Heinemann.

Greene, R. W., Abidin, R. R., & Kmetz, C. (1997). The index of teaching stress: A measure of student-teacher compatibility. *Journal of School Psychology, 35,* 239–259.

Greene, R. W., Beszterczey, S. K., Katzenstein, T., Park, K., & Goring, J. (2002). Are students with ADHD more stressful to teach? Patterns of teacher stress in an elementary school sample. *Journal of Emotional and Behavioral Disorders, 10,* 79–90.

Guglielmi, R. S., & Tatrow, K. (1998). Occupational stress, burnout and health in teachers: A methodological and theoretical analysis. *Review of Educational Research, 68,* 61–99.

Harden, R. M. (1999). Stress, pressure and burnout in teachers: Is the swan exhausted? *Medical Teacher, 21,* 245–248.

Holmes, R., & Webb, M. (1995). *The positive stress factor* (Rev. ed.). Indiana, PA: Lee Ross.

Houghton, P. (2001). Finding allies. *Phi Delta Kappan, 82,* 706.

Jacobsson, C., Pousette, A., & Thylefors, I. (2001). Managing stress and feelings of mastery among Swedish comprehensive school teachers. *Scandinavian Journal of Educational Research, 45,* 37–53.

Kirchner, J. E., Yoder, M. C., Kramer, T. L., Lindsey, M. S., & Thrush, C. R. (2000). Development of an educational program to increase school personnel's awareness about child and adolescent depression. *Education, 121,* 235–247.

Krall, C. M., & Jalongo, M. R. (1998). Creating a caring community in classrooms: Advice from an intervention specialist. *Childhood Education, 75,* 83–90.

Kyriacou, C. (2000). *Stress-busting for teachers.* Cheltenham, UK: Stanley Thomas.

Kyriacou, C. (2001, February). Teacher stress: Directions for future research. *Educational Review, 53*(1), 27–36.

Kyriacou, C., & Sutcliffe, J. (1977). Teacher stress: A review. *Educational Review, 29,* 299–306.

Leatz, C., & Stolar, M. (1993). *Career success/personal stress: How to stay healthy in a high stress environment.* New York: McGraw Hill.

Levchuck, C., Kosek, J., & Drohan, M. (2000). Nutrition [Electronic version]. Healthy Living. Available from Public Library of Charlotte & Mecklenburg County, Health and Wellness Resource Center, http://www.plcmc.lib.nc.us

Loehr, J. (1997). *Stress for success.* New York: Random House.

Lozada, M. (2000). Teachers . . . be revitalized. *Techniques, 75,* 26.

Lunenburg, F. C., & Ornstein, A. C. (2000). *Educational Administration* (3rd ed.). Belmont, CA: Wadsworth/Thomson Learning.

McGrath, M. (1995). *Teachers today: A guide to surviving creatively.* Thousand Oaks, CA: Corwin Press.

Moriarty, V., Edmonds, S., Blatchford, P., & Martin, C. (2001). Teaching young children: Perceived satisfaction and stress. *Educational Research, 43,* 33–47.

Murray-Harvey, R., Slee, P. T., Lawson, M. J., Silins, H., Banfield, G., & Russell, A. (2000). Under stress: The concerns and coping strategies of teacher education students. *European Journal of Teacher Education, 23,* 19–36.

Natvig, G. M., Albrektsen, G., & Qvarnstrom, U. (2001). School-related stress experience as a risk factor for bullying behavior. *Journal of Youth and Adolescence, 30,* 561–675.

No child left behind—Frequently asked questions. Retrieved May 23, 2002, from http://www.ncpublicschools.org/nclb/

Nutrition and stress, fact sheet. (n.d.). Clemson University, College of Agriculture, Forestry and Life Sciences, Nutrition Information Resource Center.

O'Neill, T. (2002, October, 7). Post-traumatic school disorder. *Report/Newsmagazine* (National Edition), *29*(19), 51–54.

Piekaraska, A. (2000). School stress, teachers' abusive behaviors, and children's coping strategies. *Child Abuse & Neglect, 24,* 1443–1449.

Pithers, R. T., & Soden, R. (1998). Scottish and Australian teacher stress and strain: A comparative study. *British Journal of Educational Psychology, 68,* 269–279.

Powell, R. (1994). *The working woman's guide to managing stress.* Englewood Cliffs, NJ: Prentice Hall.

Romano, J. L., & Wahlstrom, K. (2000). Professional stress and well-being of K-12 teachers in alternative educational settings: A leadership agenda. *Leadership in Education, 3,* 121–135.

Sternberg, R. E. (2001). The ultimate stress. *School Administrator, 58,* 6–9.

Streisand, B., & Tote, T. (1998, September 14). Many millions of kids, and too few teachers: Across America, teaching jobs go wanting. *U.S. News & World Report, 125*(10), 24–25.

Torsheim, T., & Wold, B. (2001, May). School-related stress, school support, and somatic complaints: A general population study. *Journal of Adolescent Research, 16*(3), 293–304.

Travers, C. J., & Cooper, C. L. (1996). *Teachers under pressure: Stress in the teaching profession.* London: Rutledge.

Turkington, C. (1998). *Stress management for busy people.* New York: McGraw-Hill.

Vandenberghe, R., & Huberman, A. M. (Eds.). (1999). *Understanding and preventing teacher burnout: A sourcebook of international research and practice.* Cambridge, UK: Cambridge University Press.

Van Der Linde, C. (2000, Winter). The teacher's stress and its implications for the school as an organization: How can TQM help? *Education, 121*(2), 375–383.

Wanko, M. (1995). Cut stress now. *Education Digest, 60*(7), 40–42

Wenz-Gross, M., & Siperstein, G. N. (1998). Students with learning problems at risk in middle school: Stress, social support, and adjustment. *Exceptional Children, 65,* 91–101.

Wiley, C. (2000). A synthesis of research on the causes, effects, and reduction strategies of teacher stress. *Journal of Instructional Psychology, 27,* 80–88.

Williams, J. (1997). How I fought teacher burnout with good nutrition. *Instructor, 107,* 96(1).

**CORWIN
PRESS**

The Corwin Press logo—a raven striding across an open book—represents the union of courage and learning. Corwin Press is committed to improving education for all learners by publishing books and other professional development resources for those serving the field of K–12 education. By providing practical, hands-on materials, Corwin Press continues to carry out the promise of its motto: **"Helping Educators Do Their Work Better."**